Coloring book for adults relaxation

I0477639

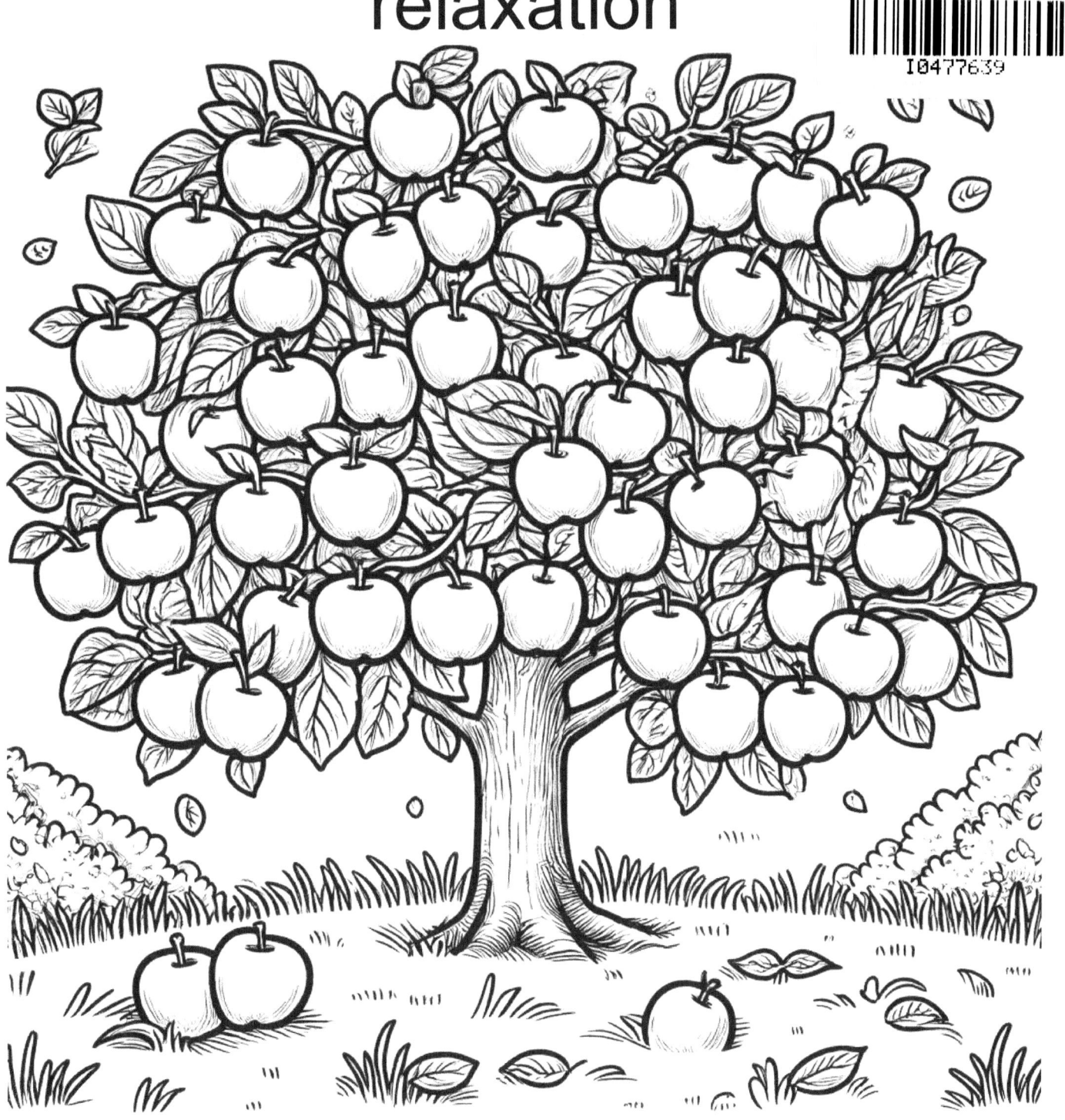

For ages 12-18

Pérez Arboleda

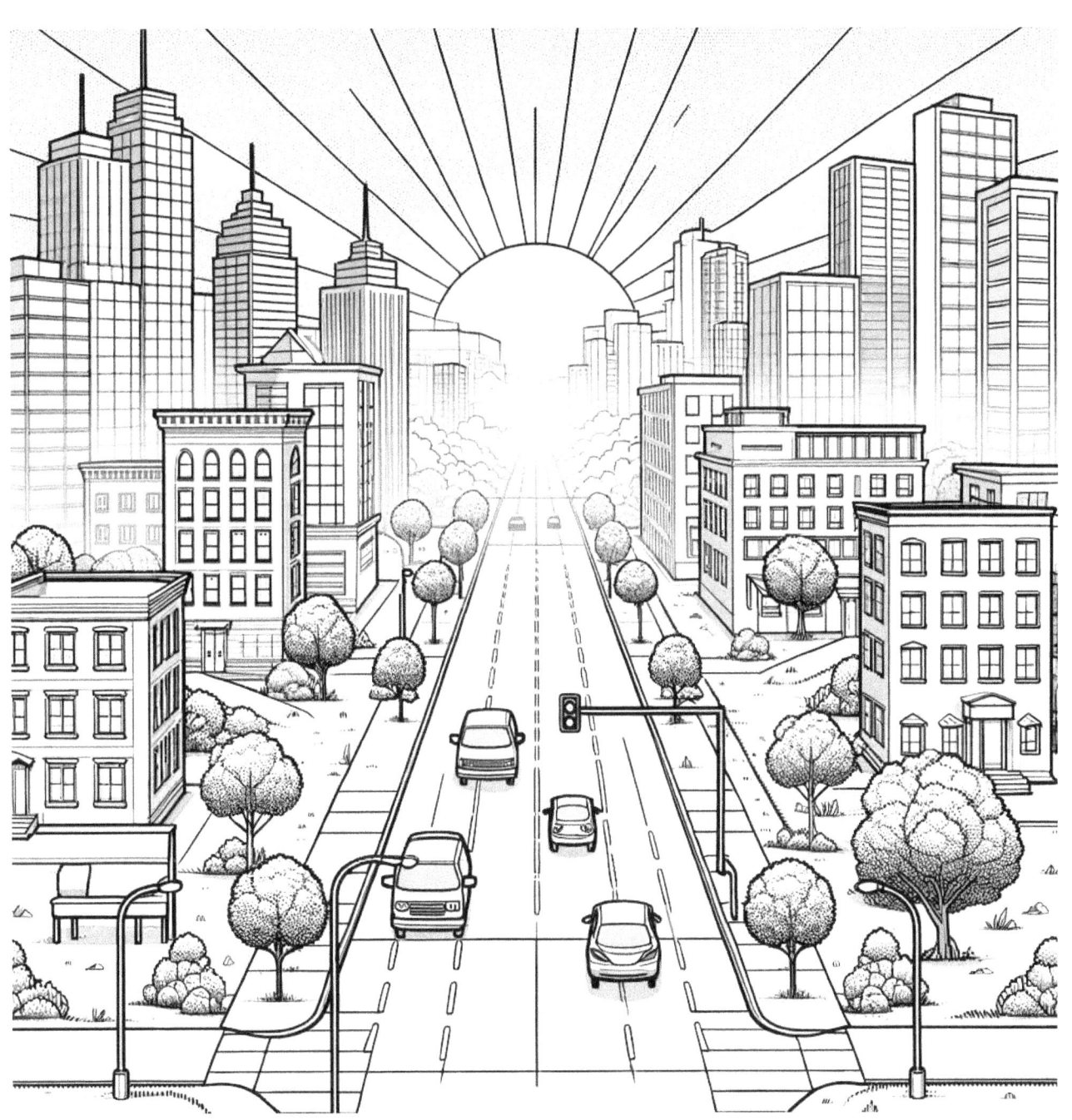

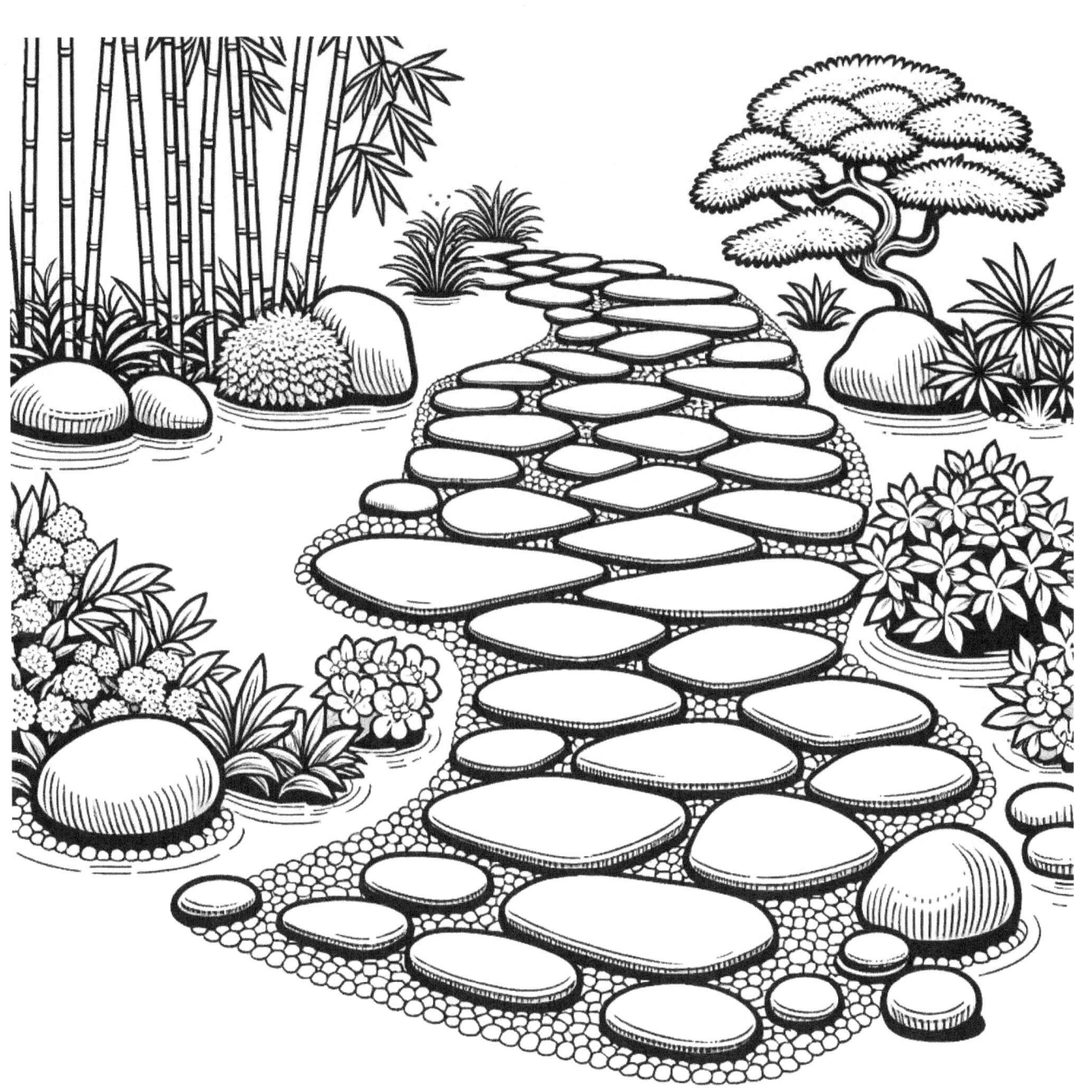

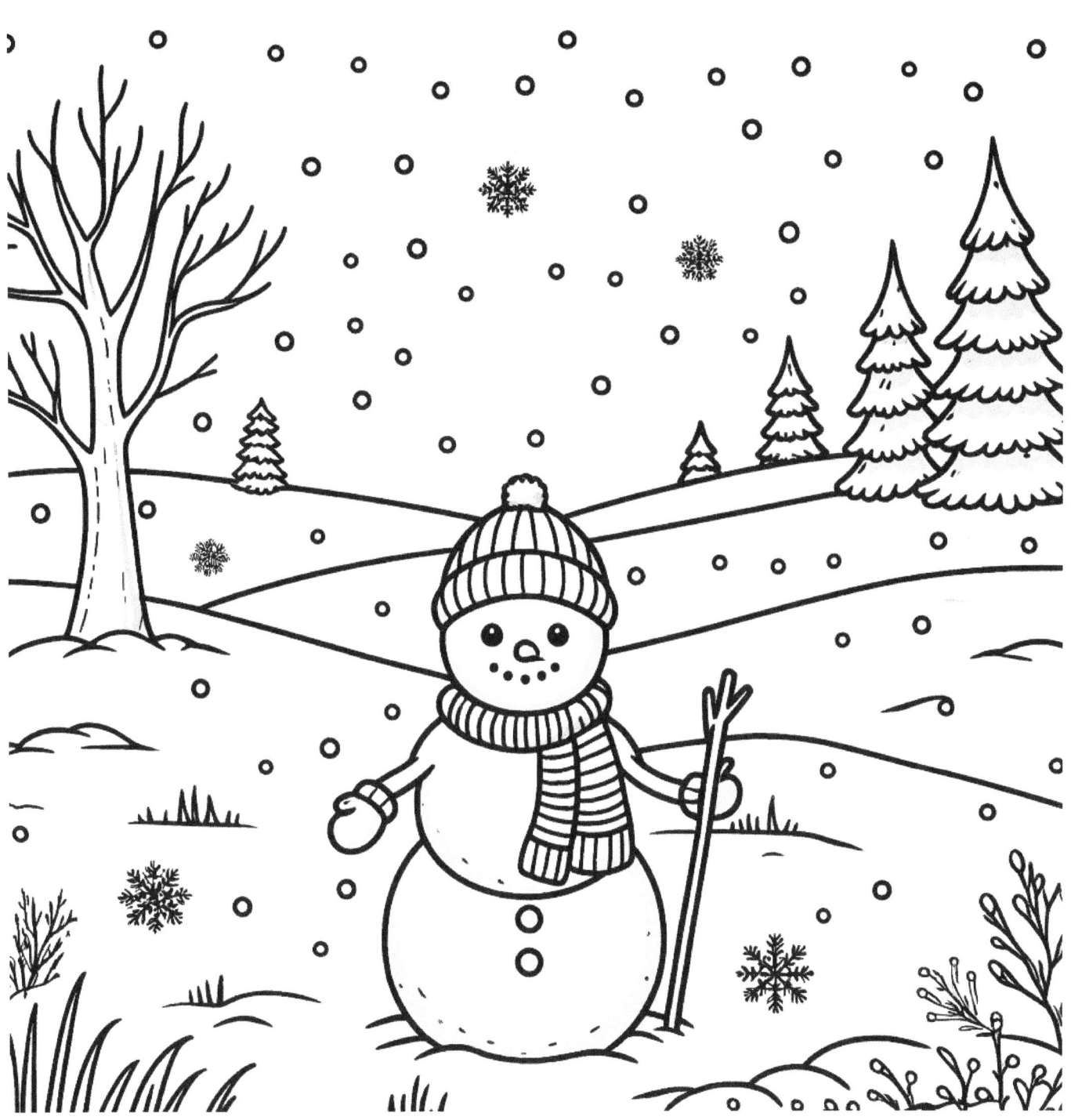

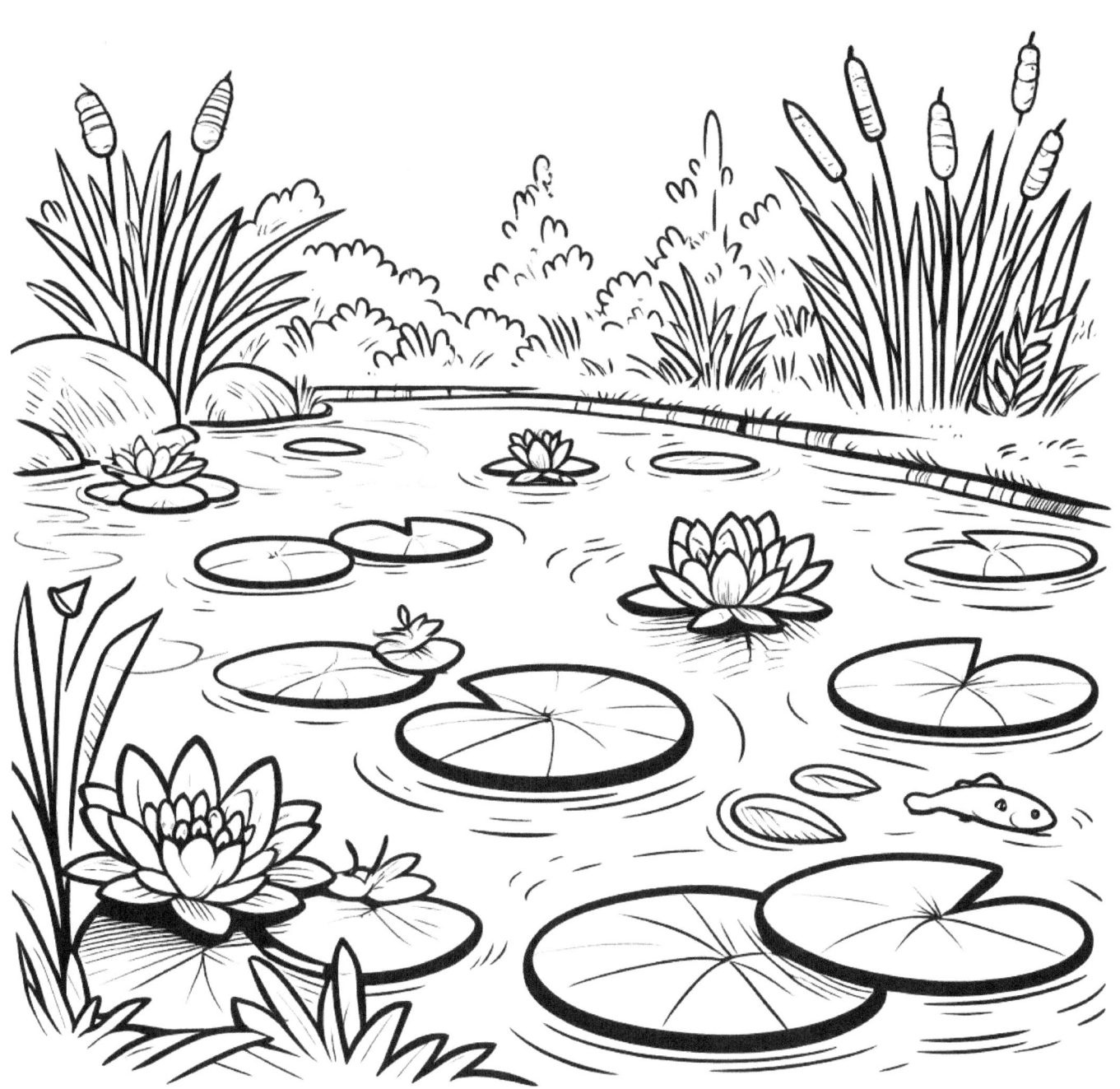

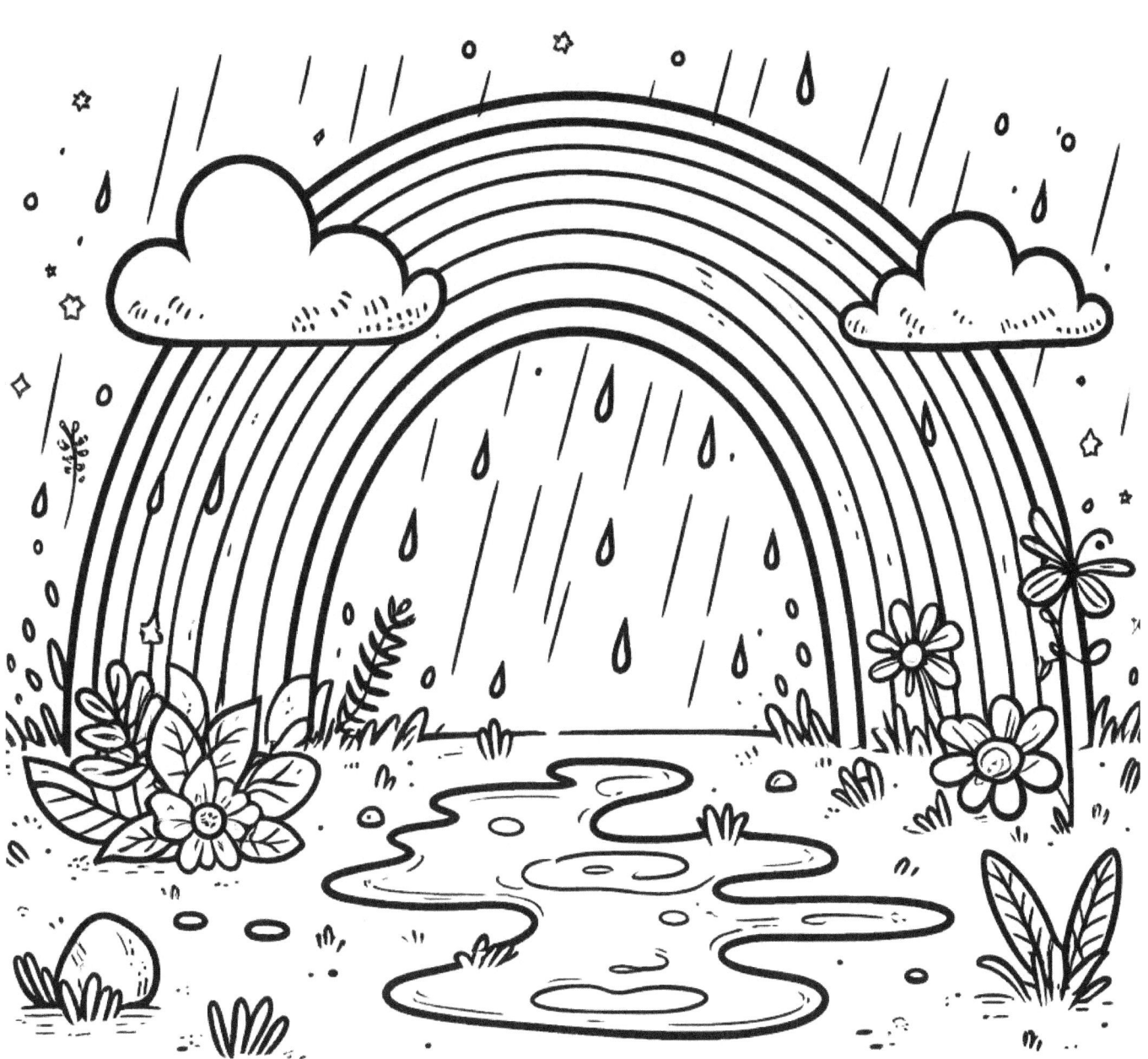

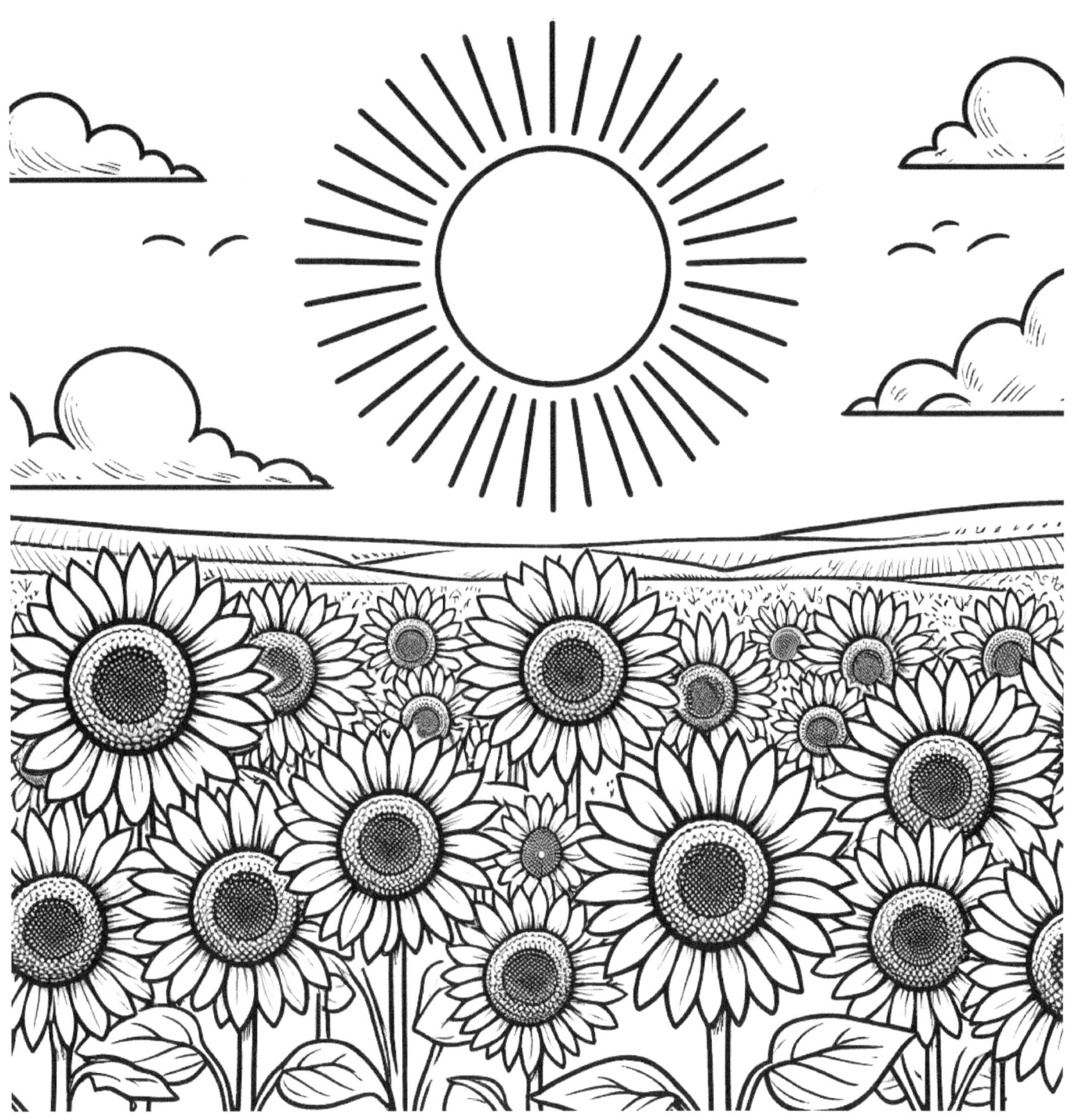

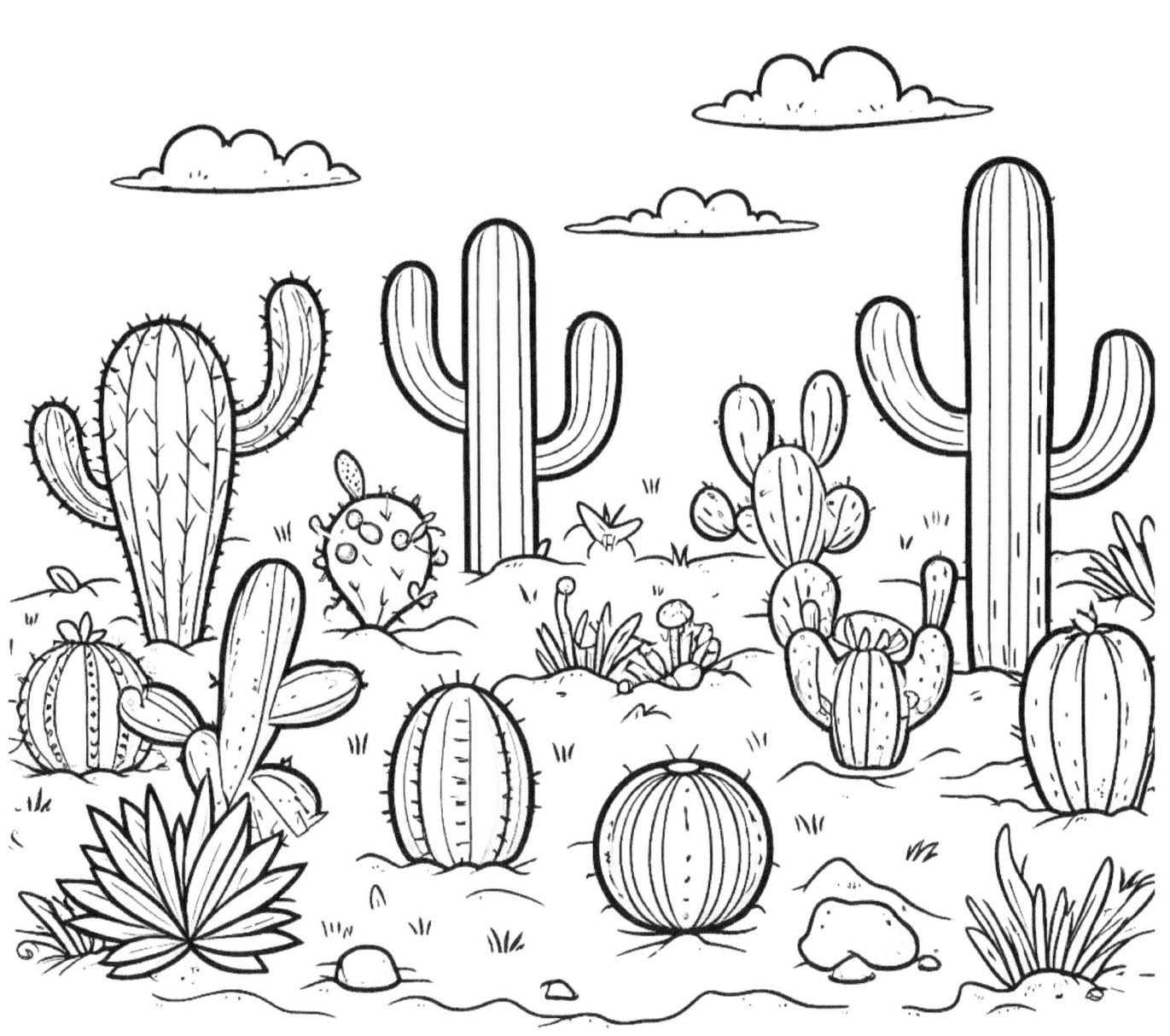

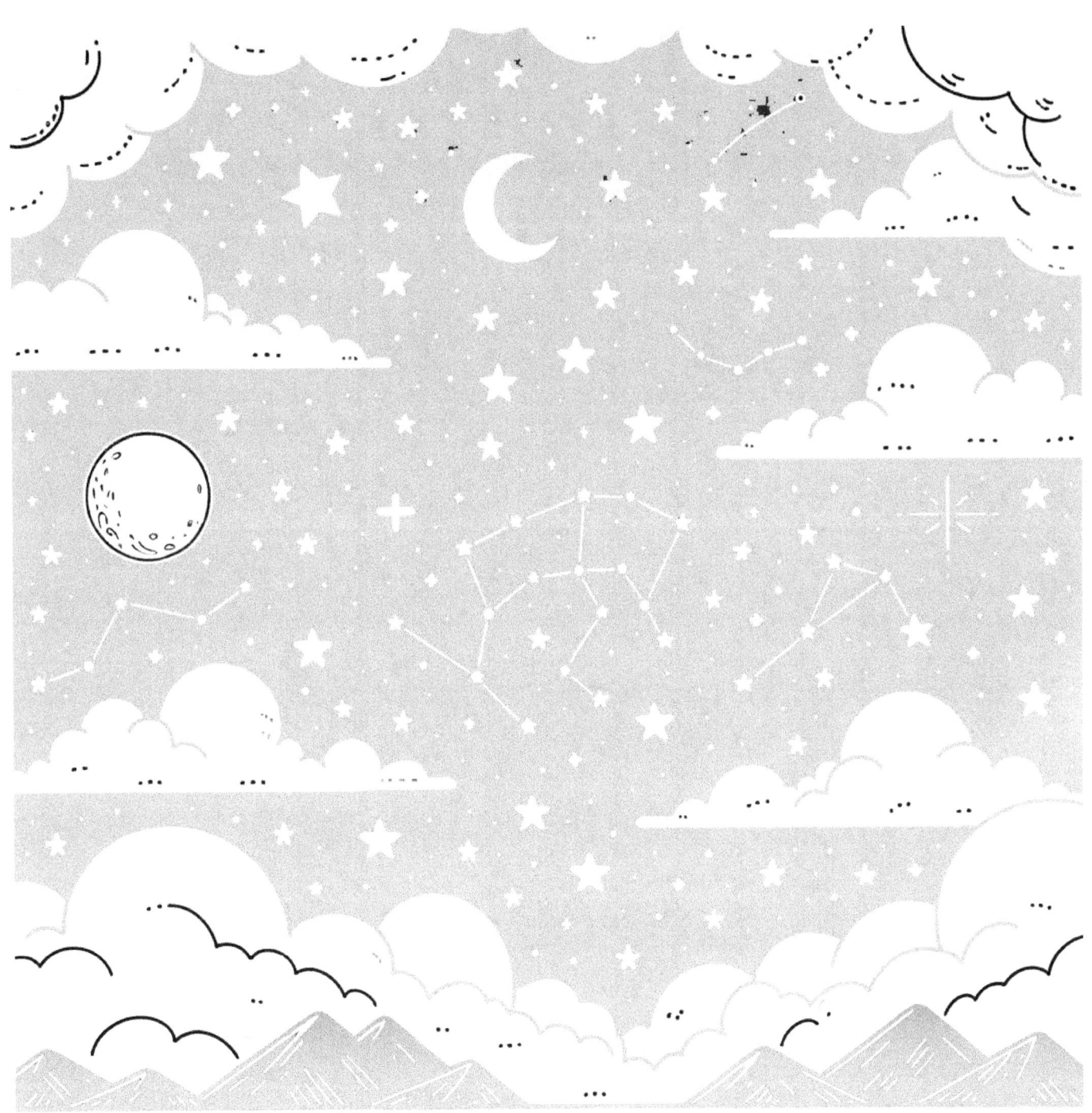

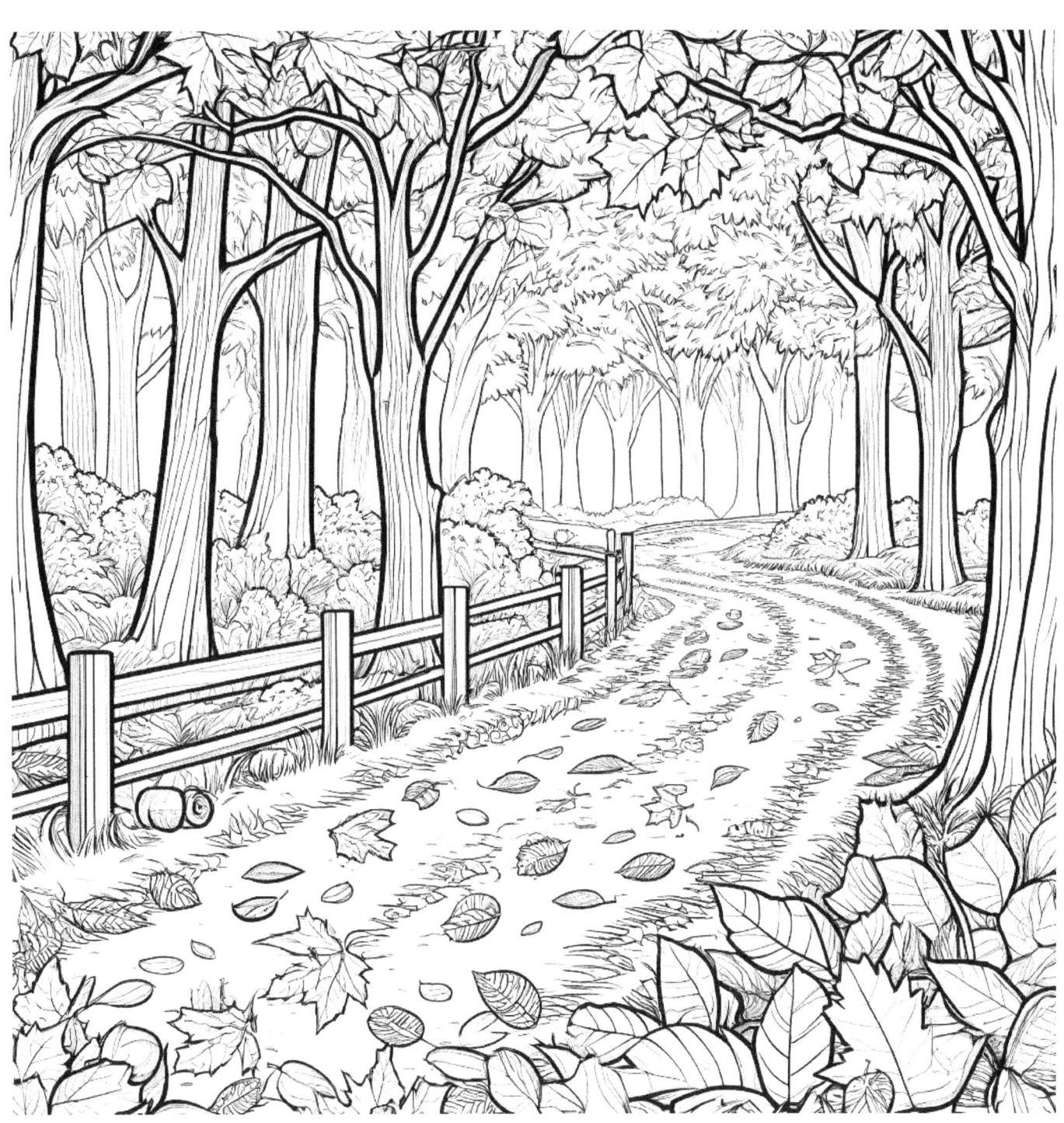

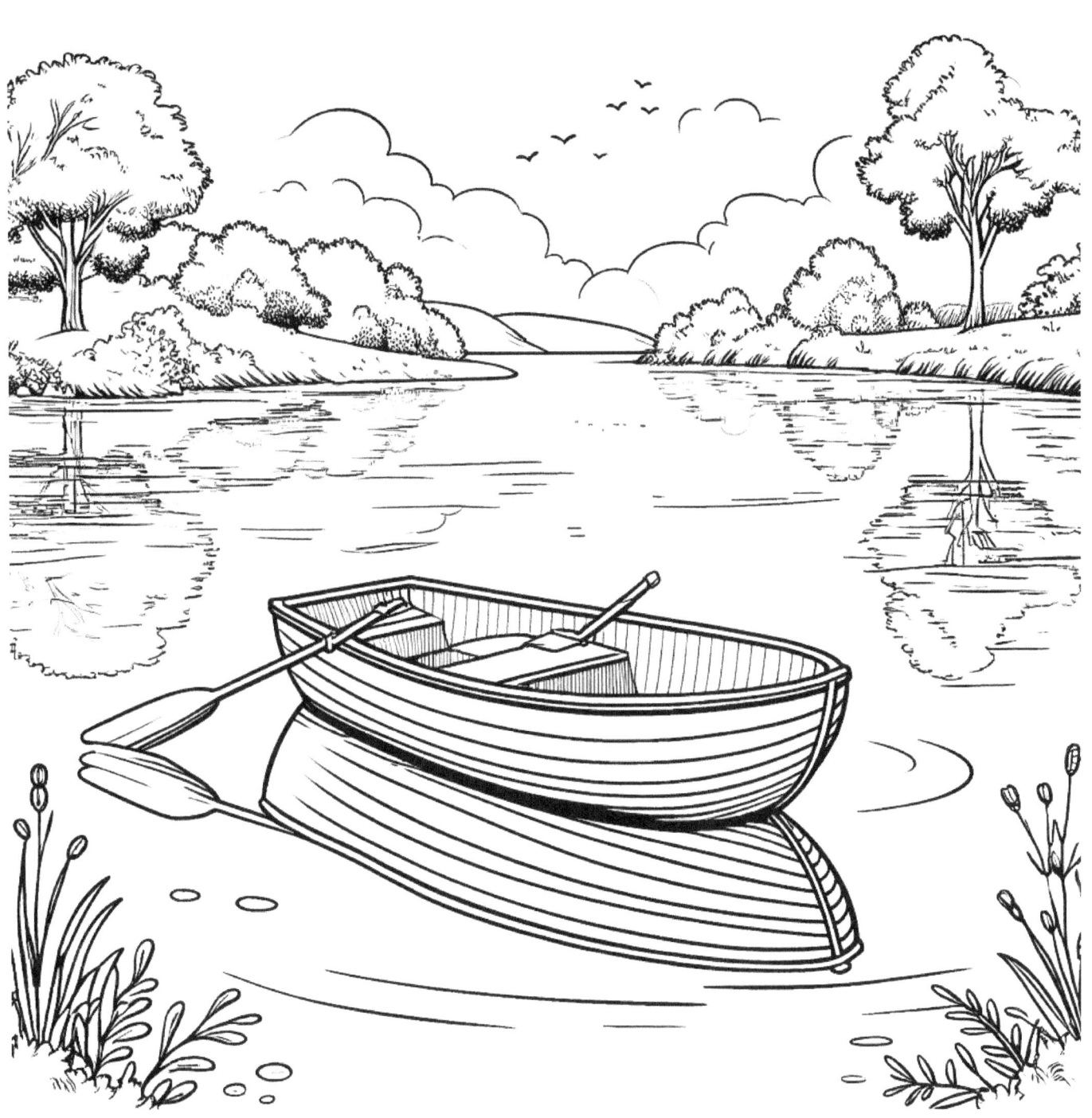

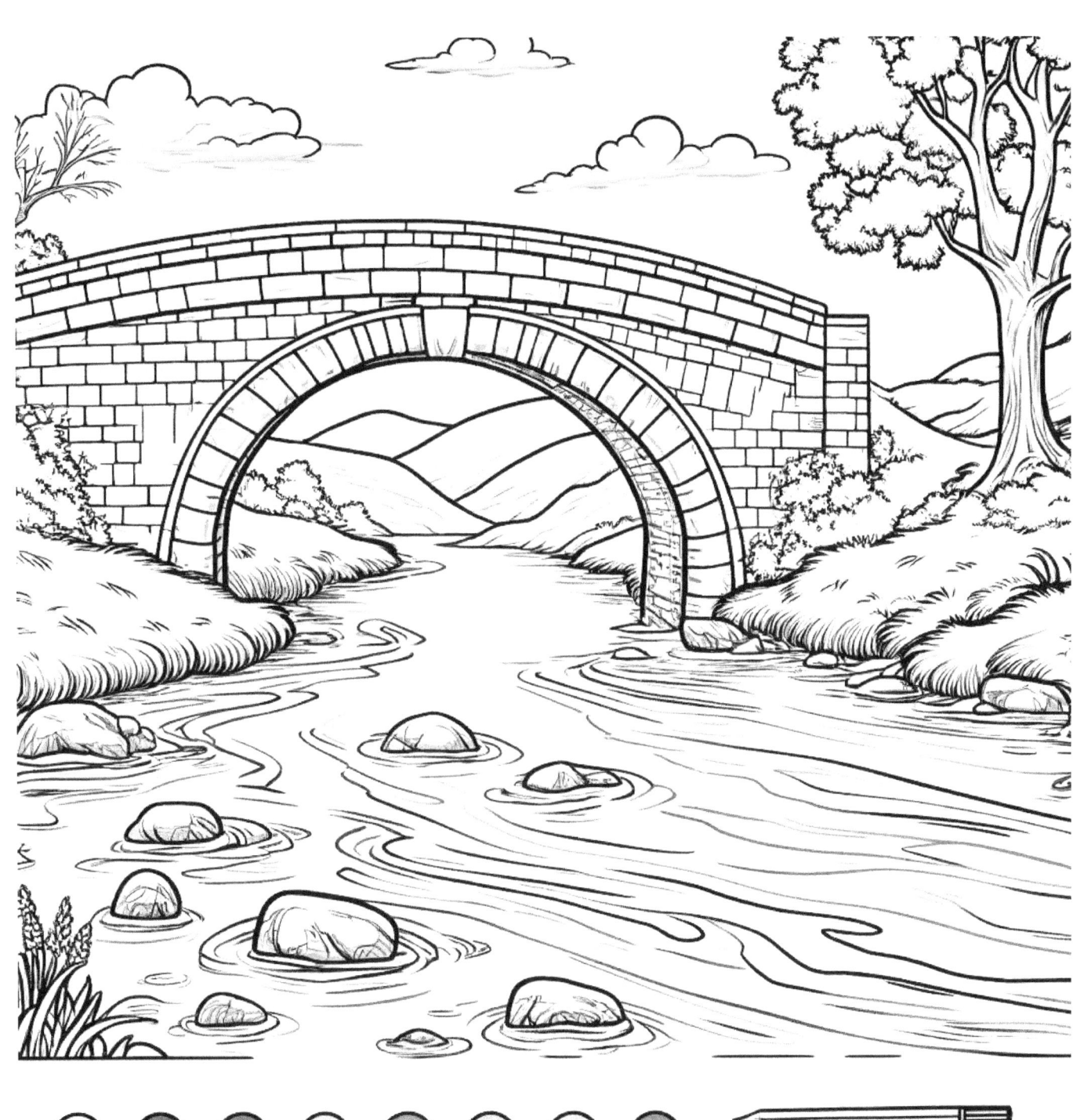

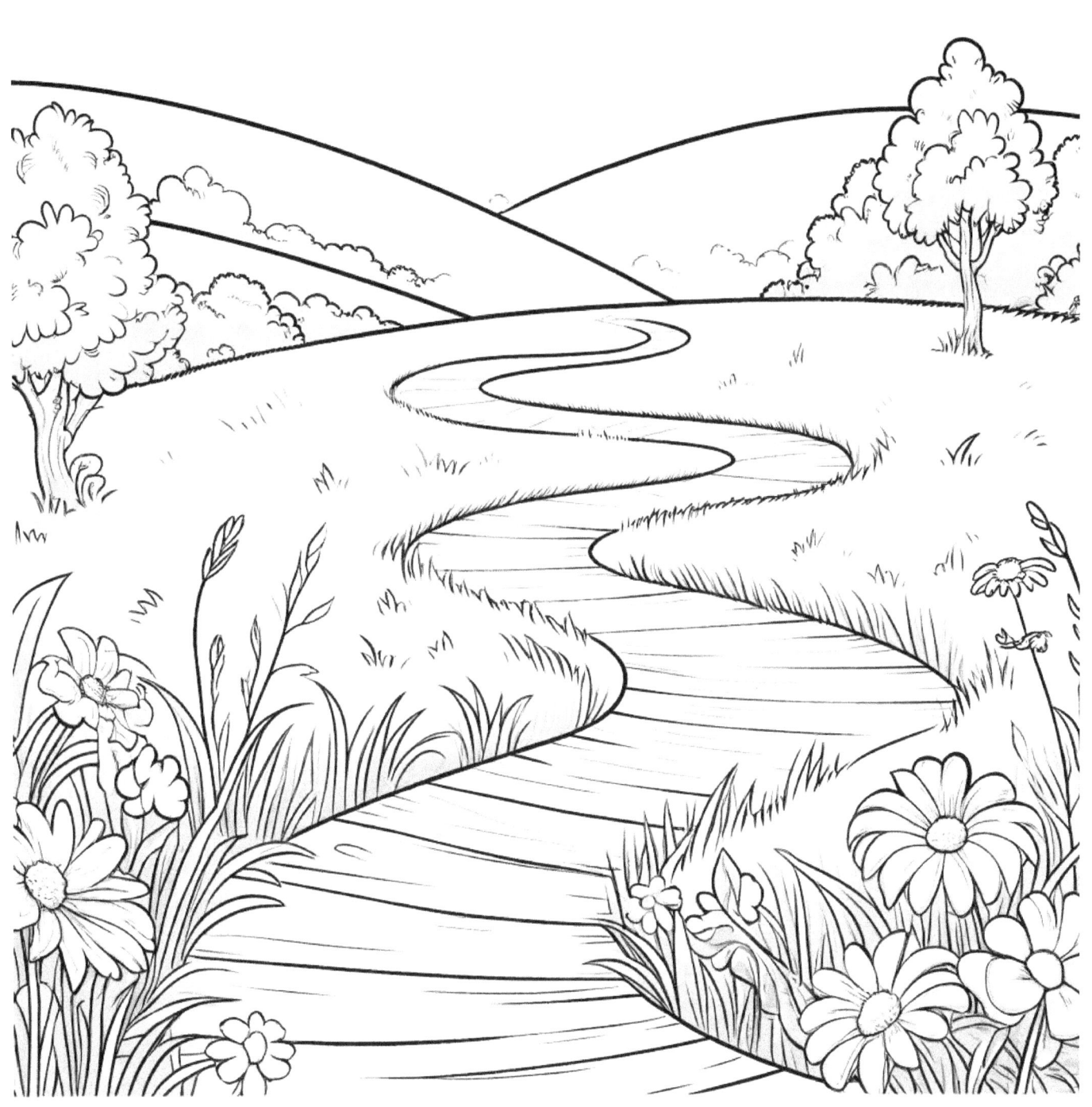

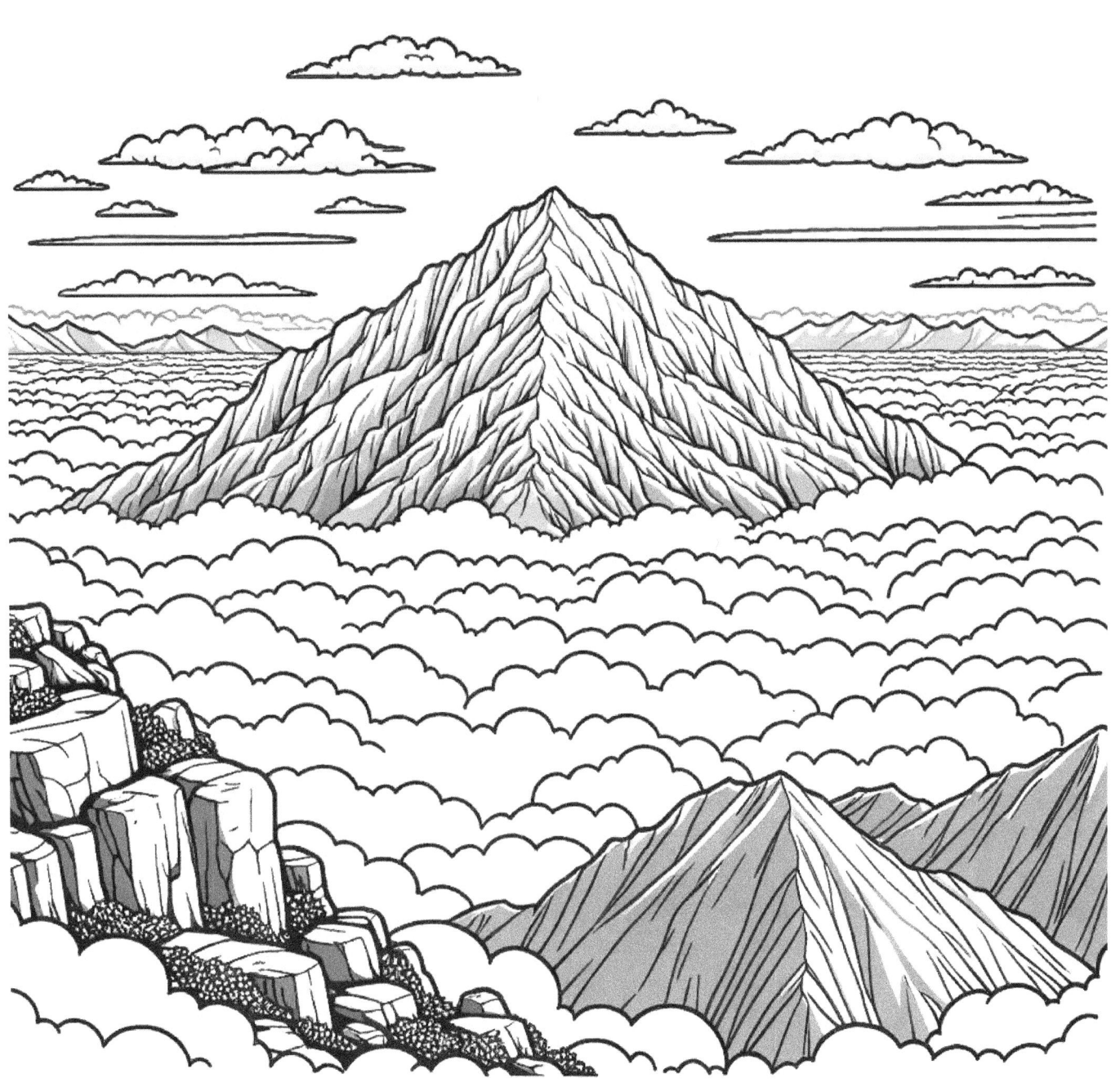

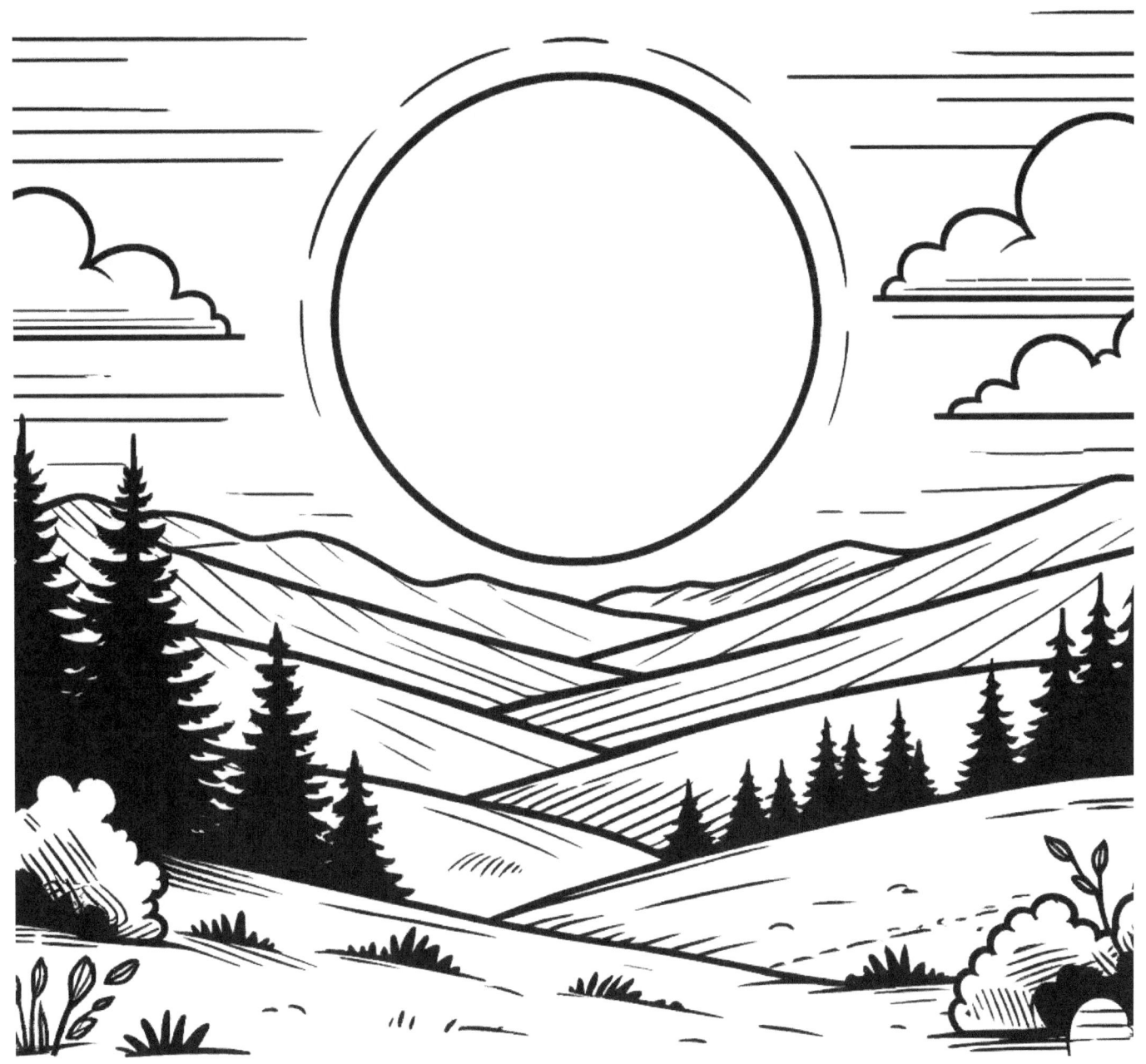

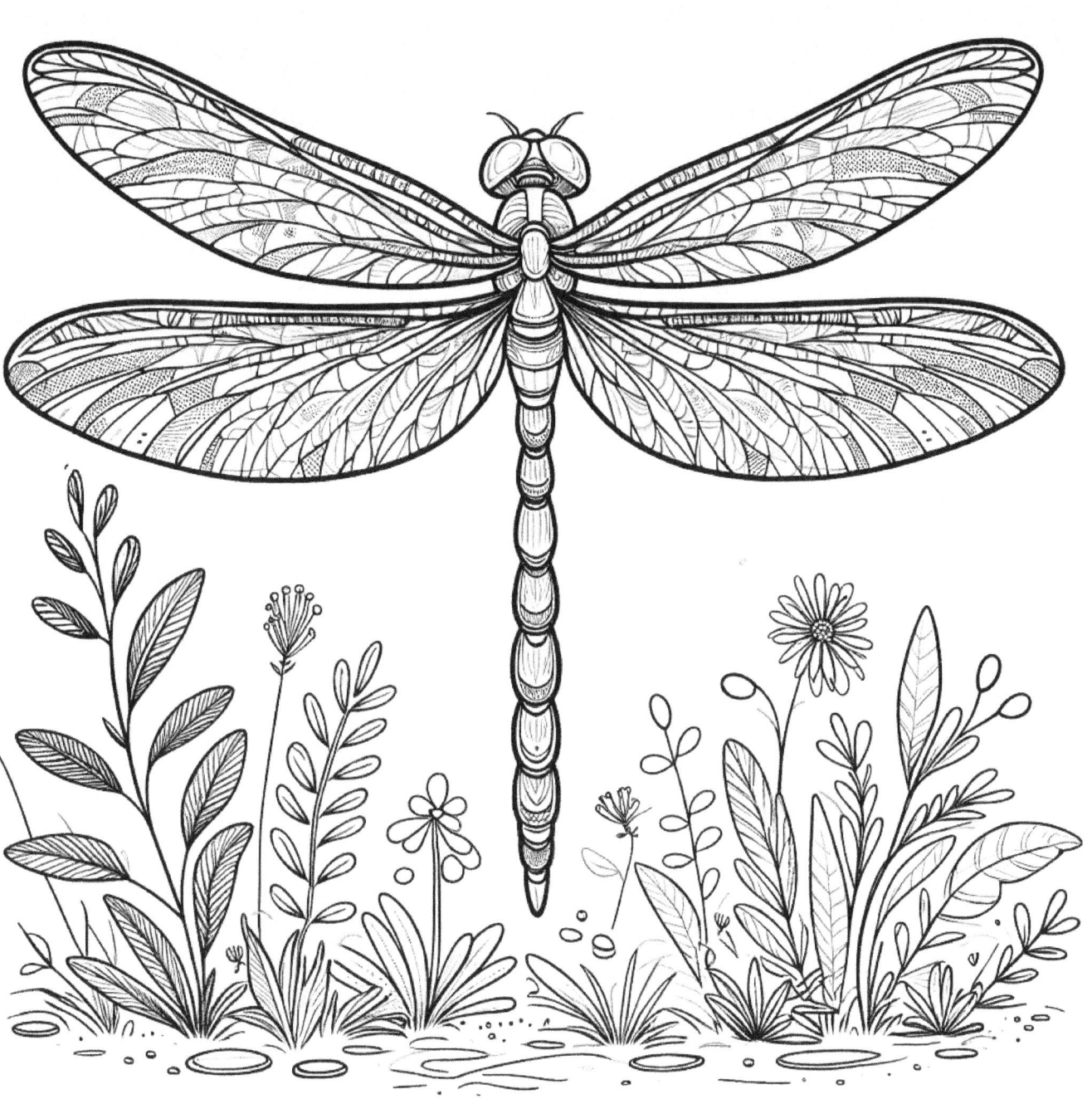

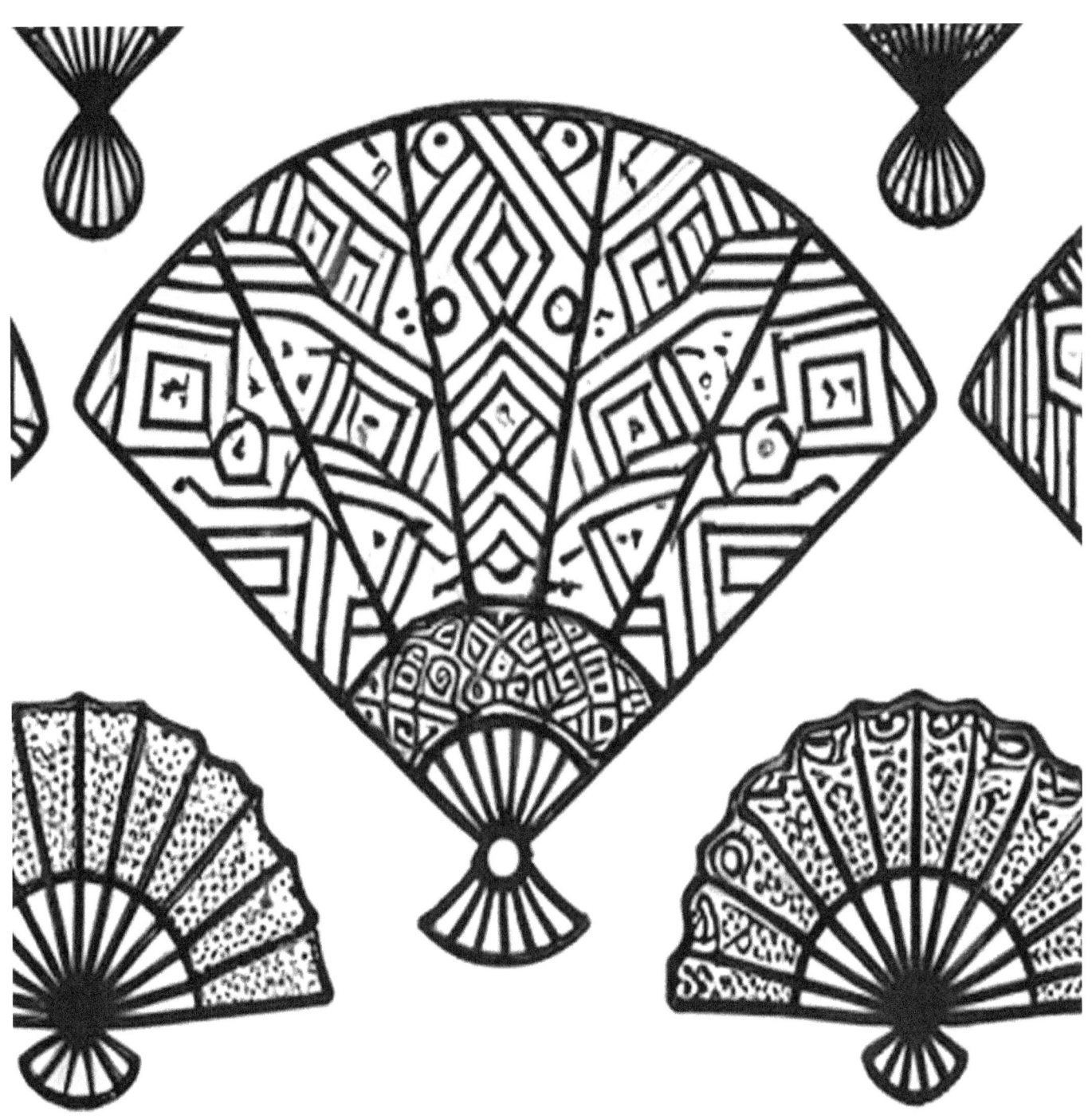

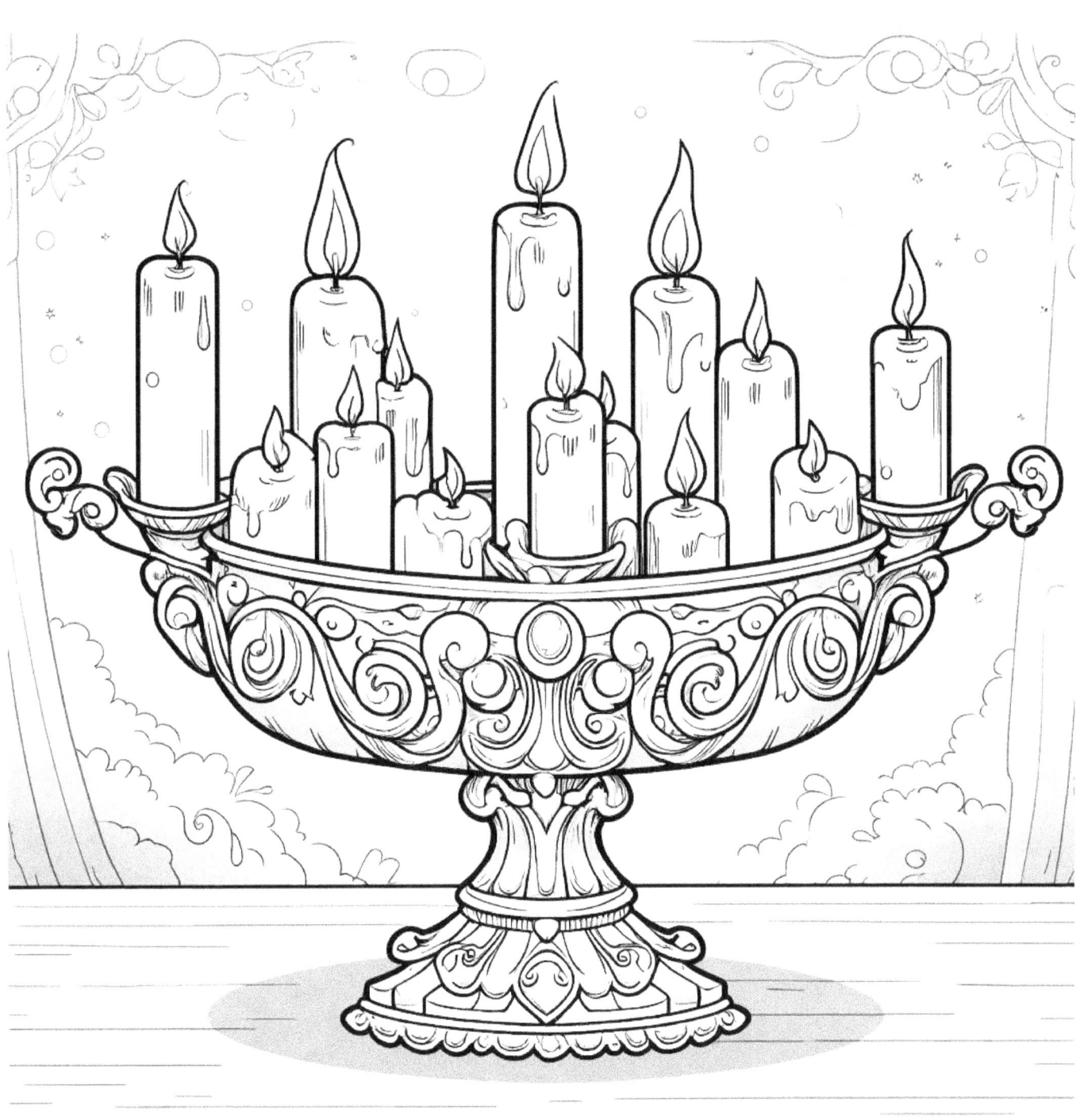

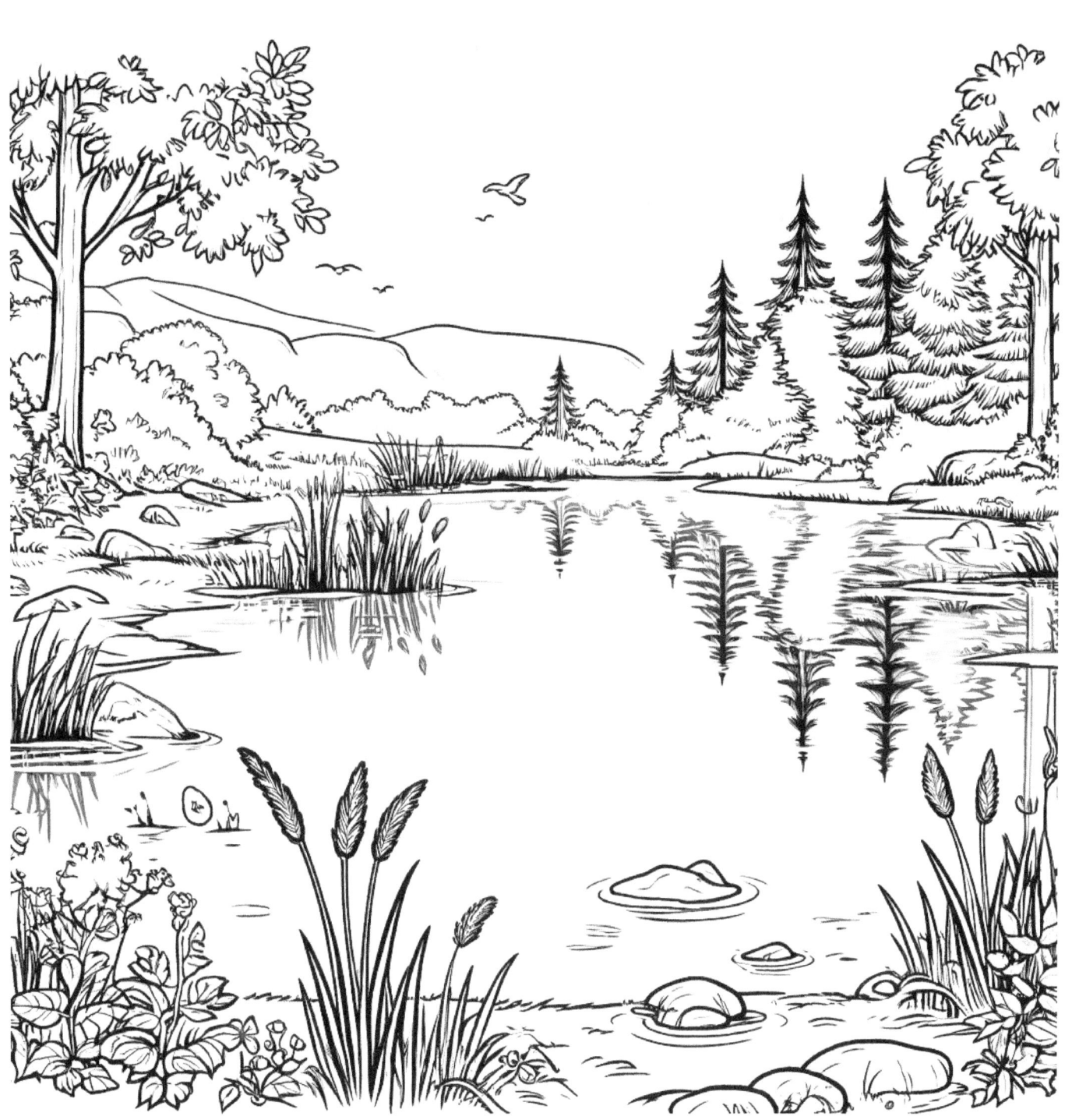

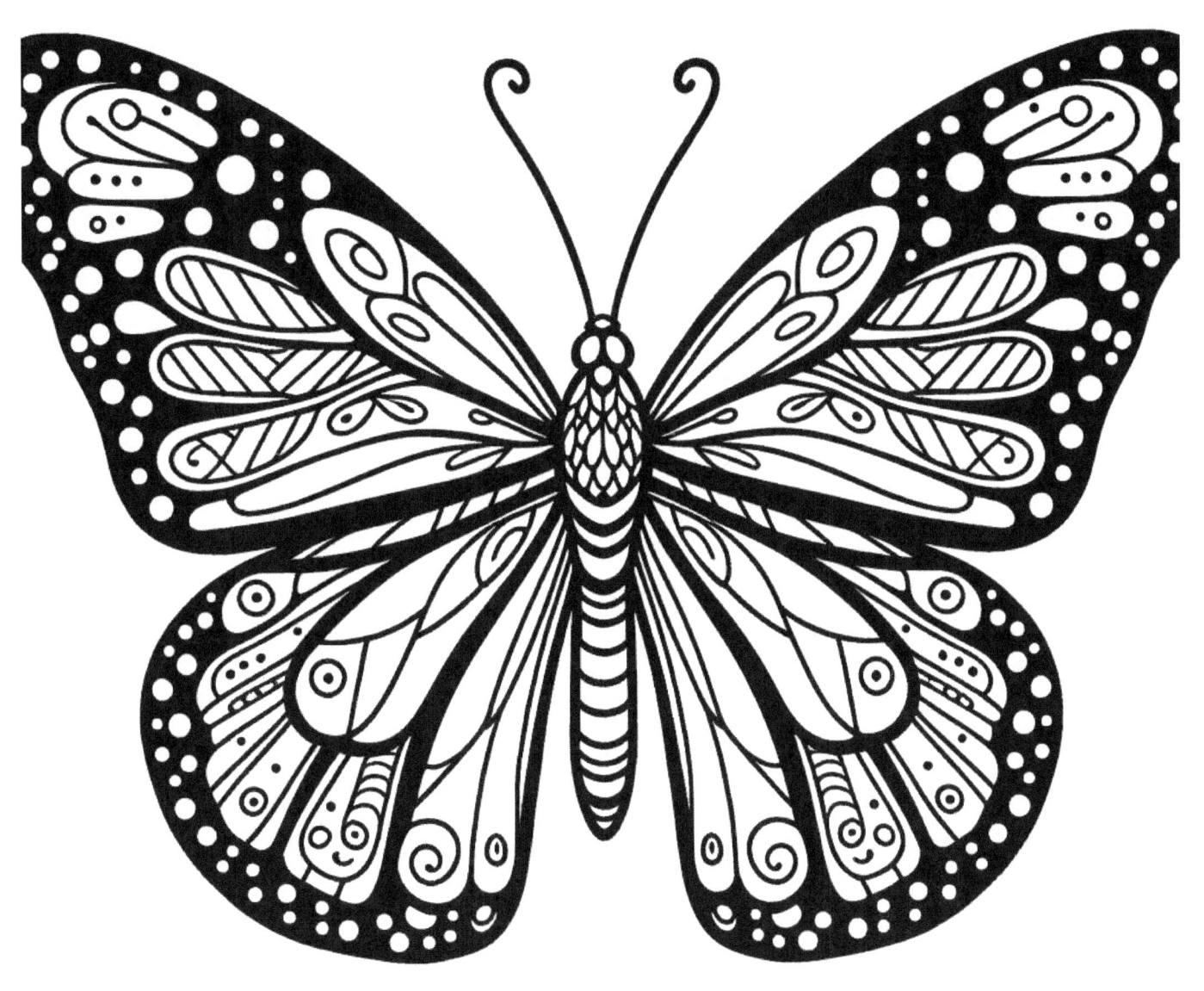

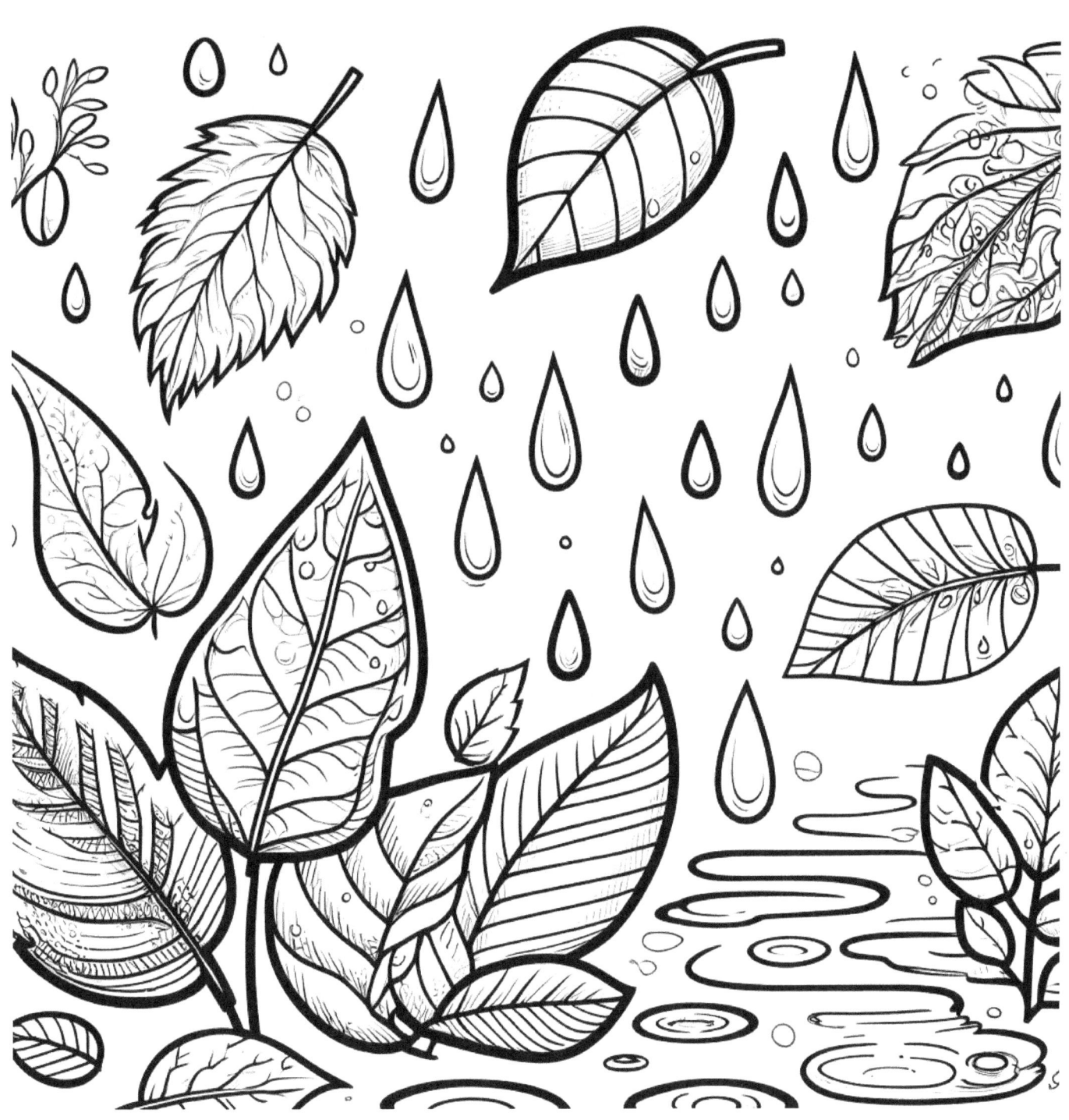

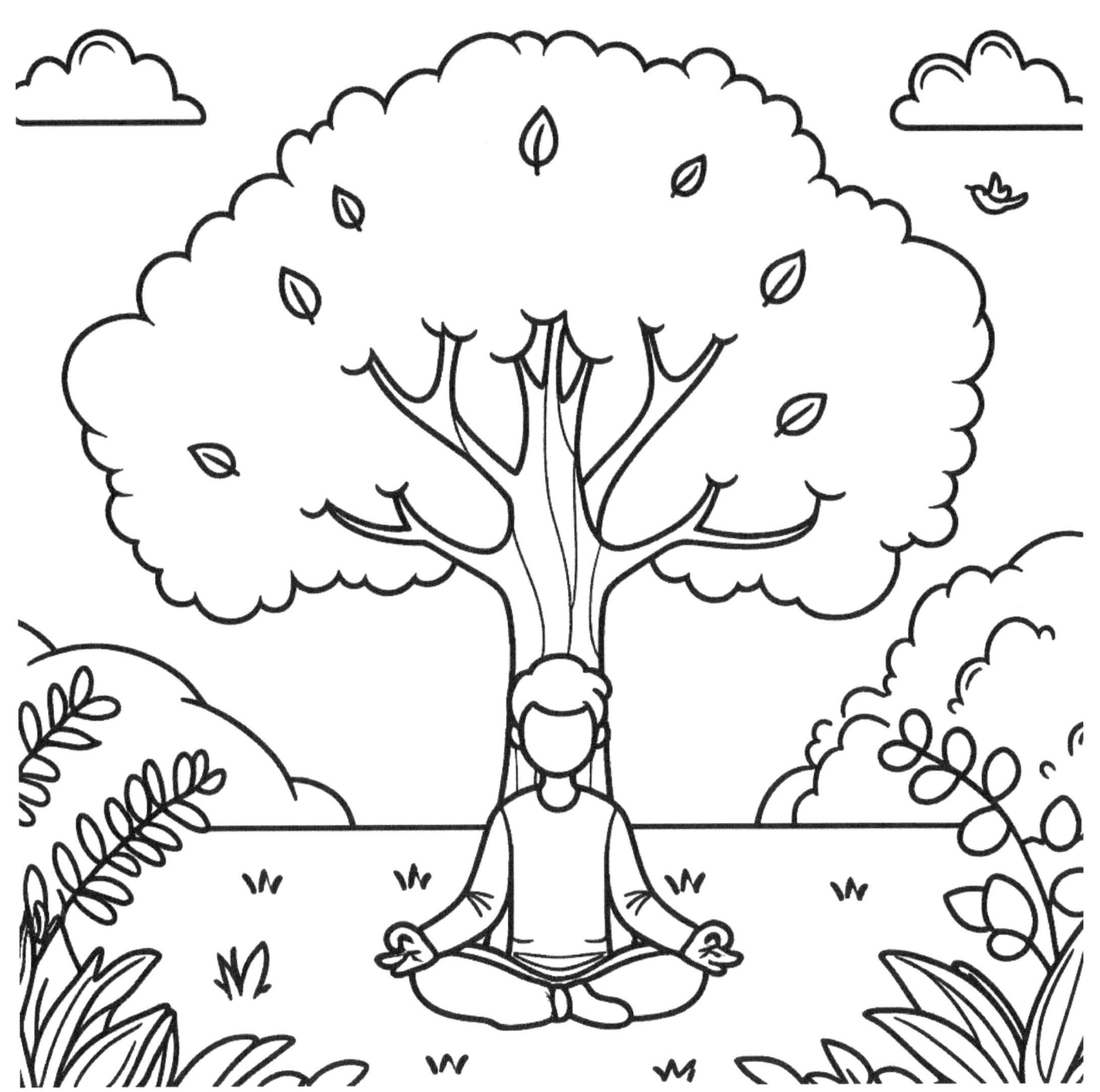

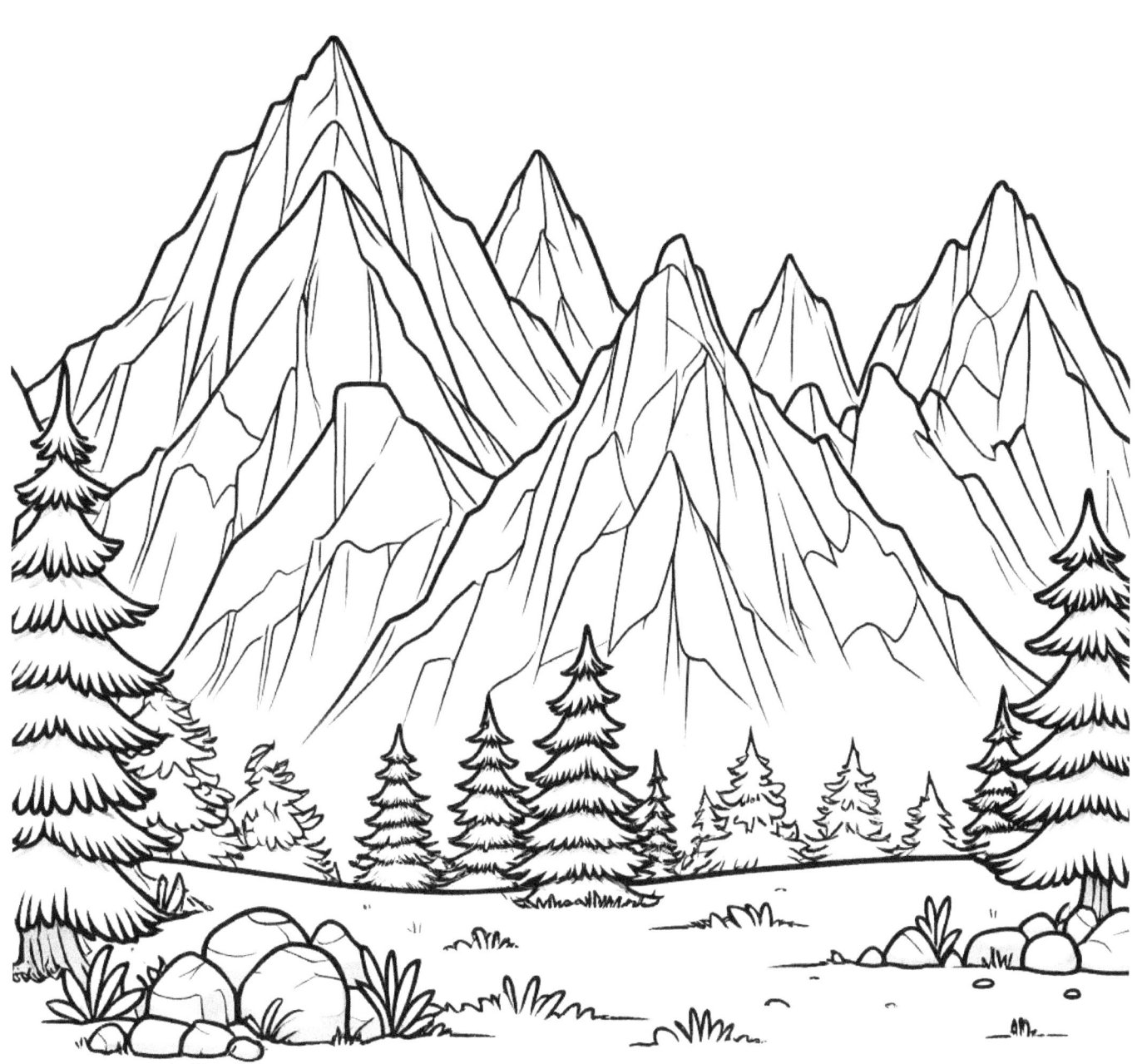

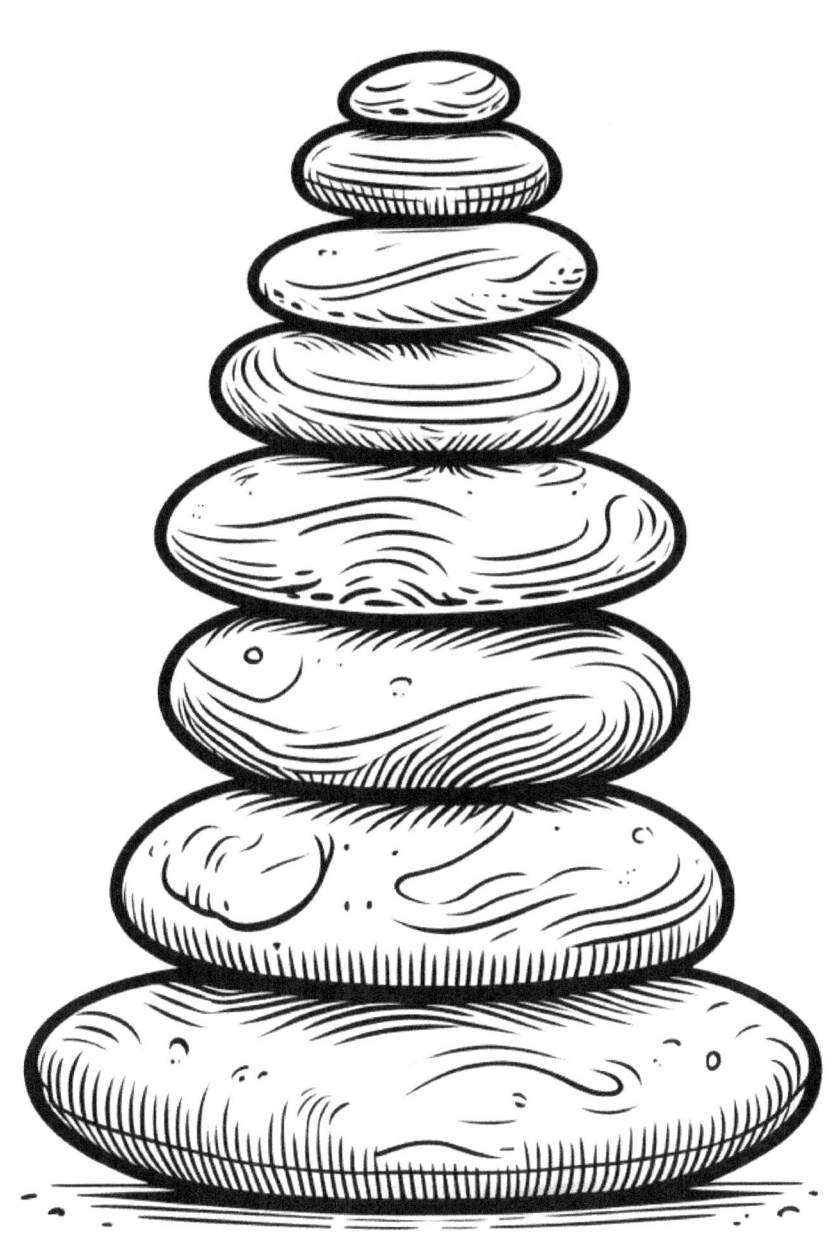

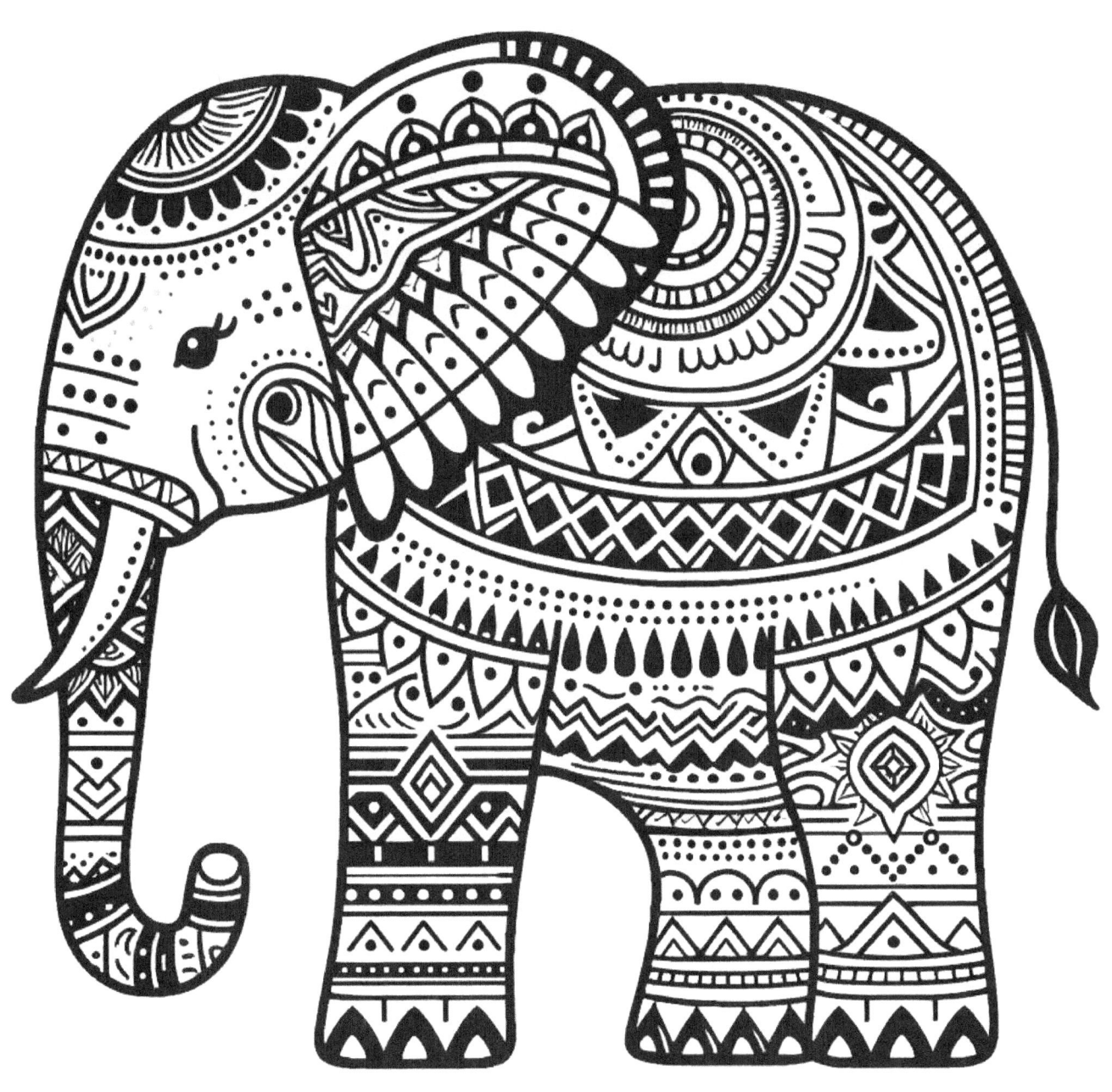

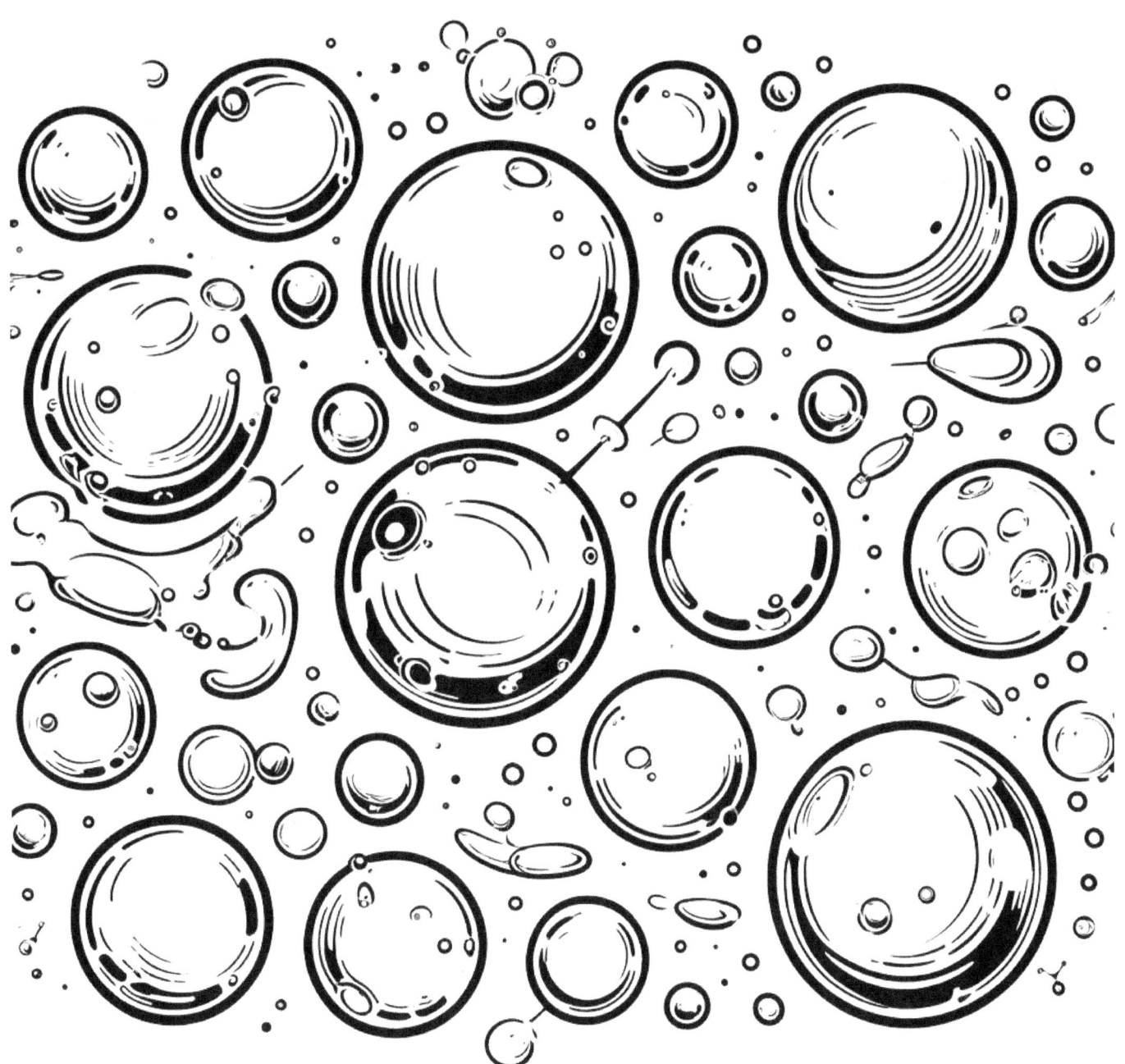

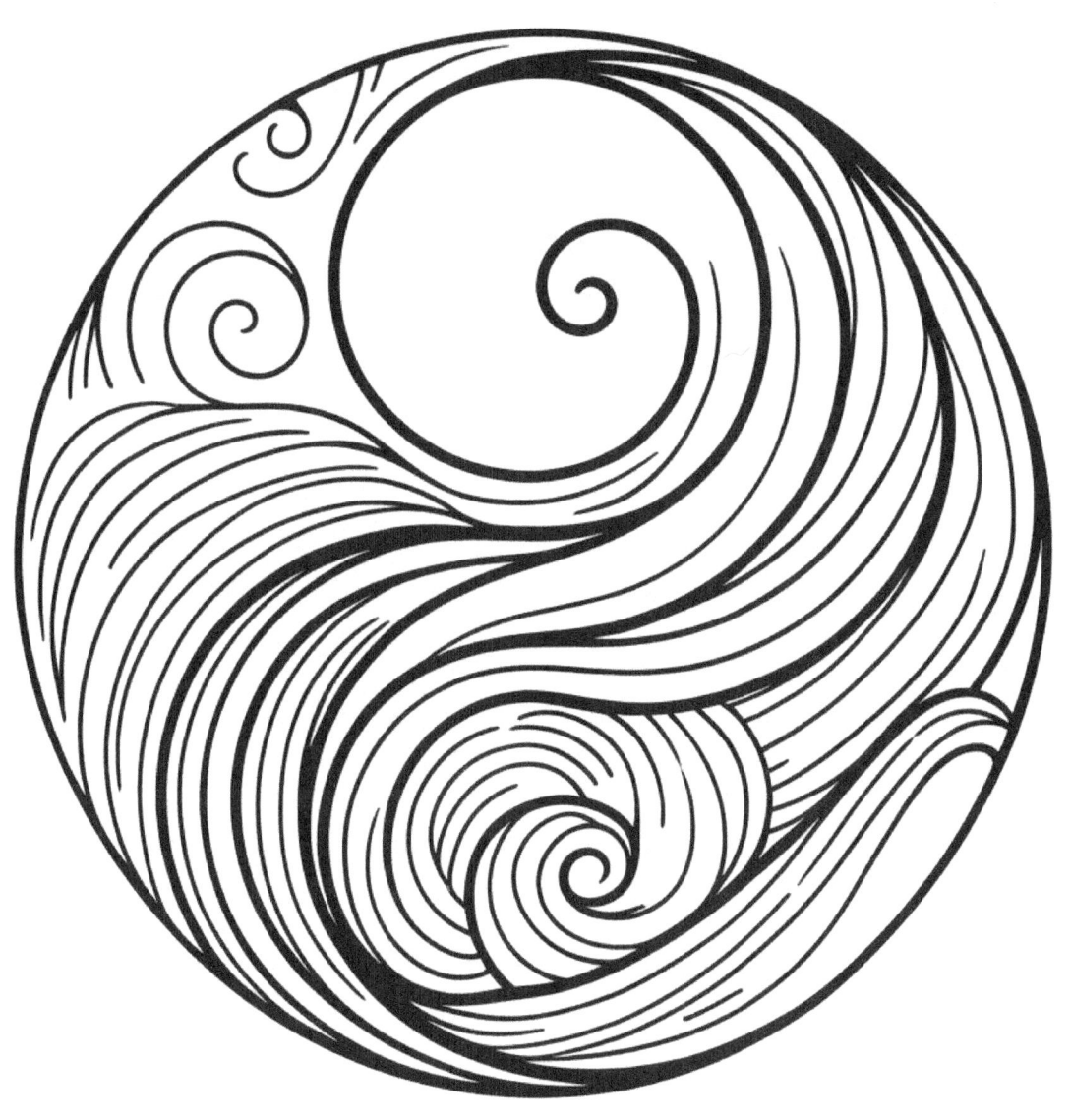

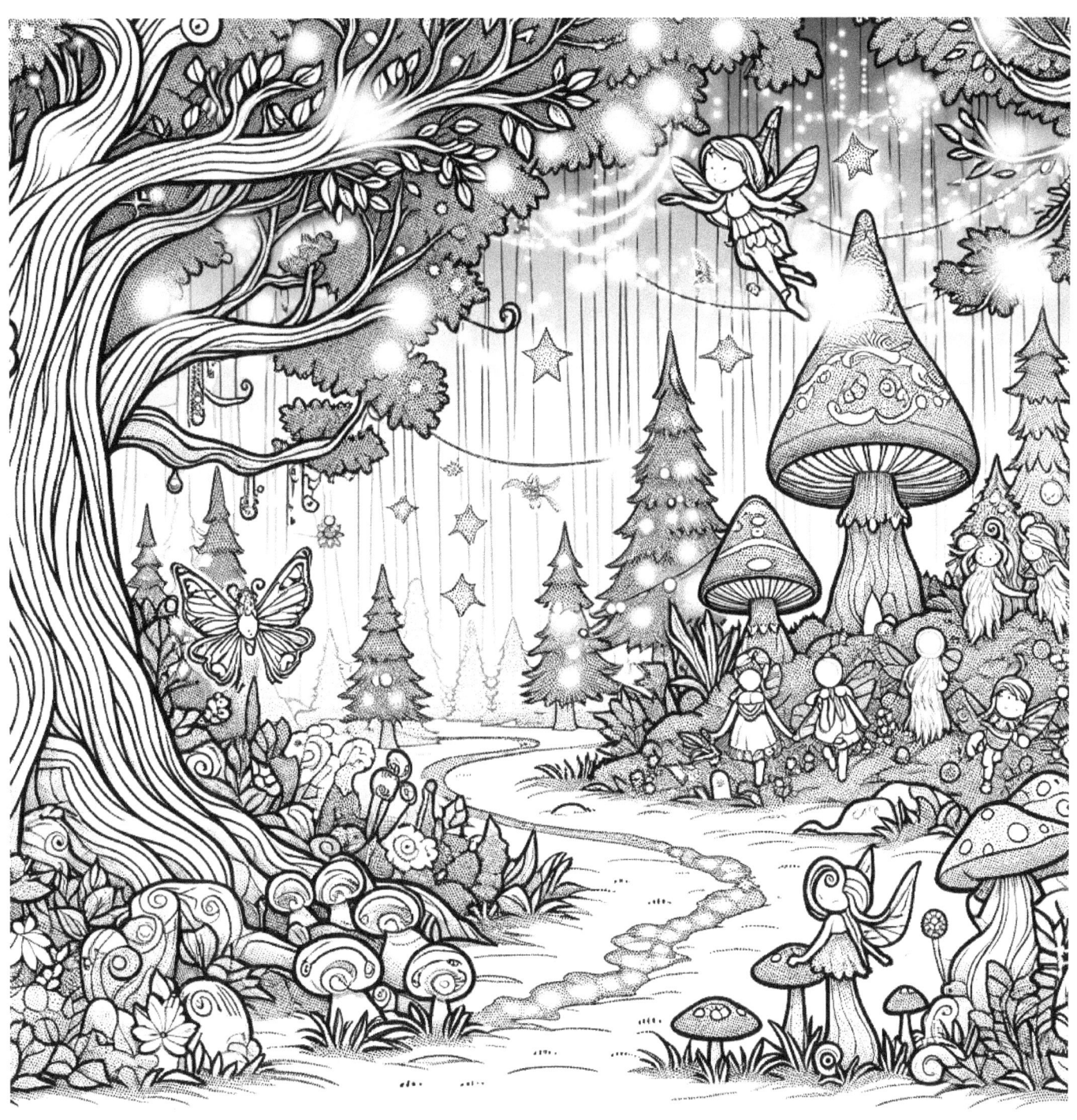

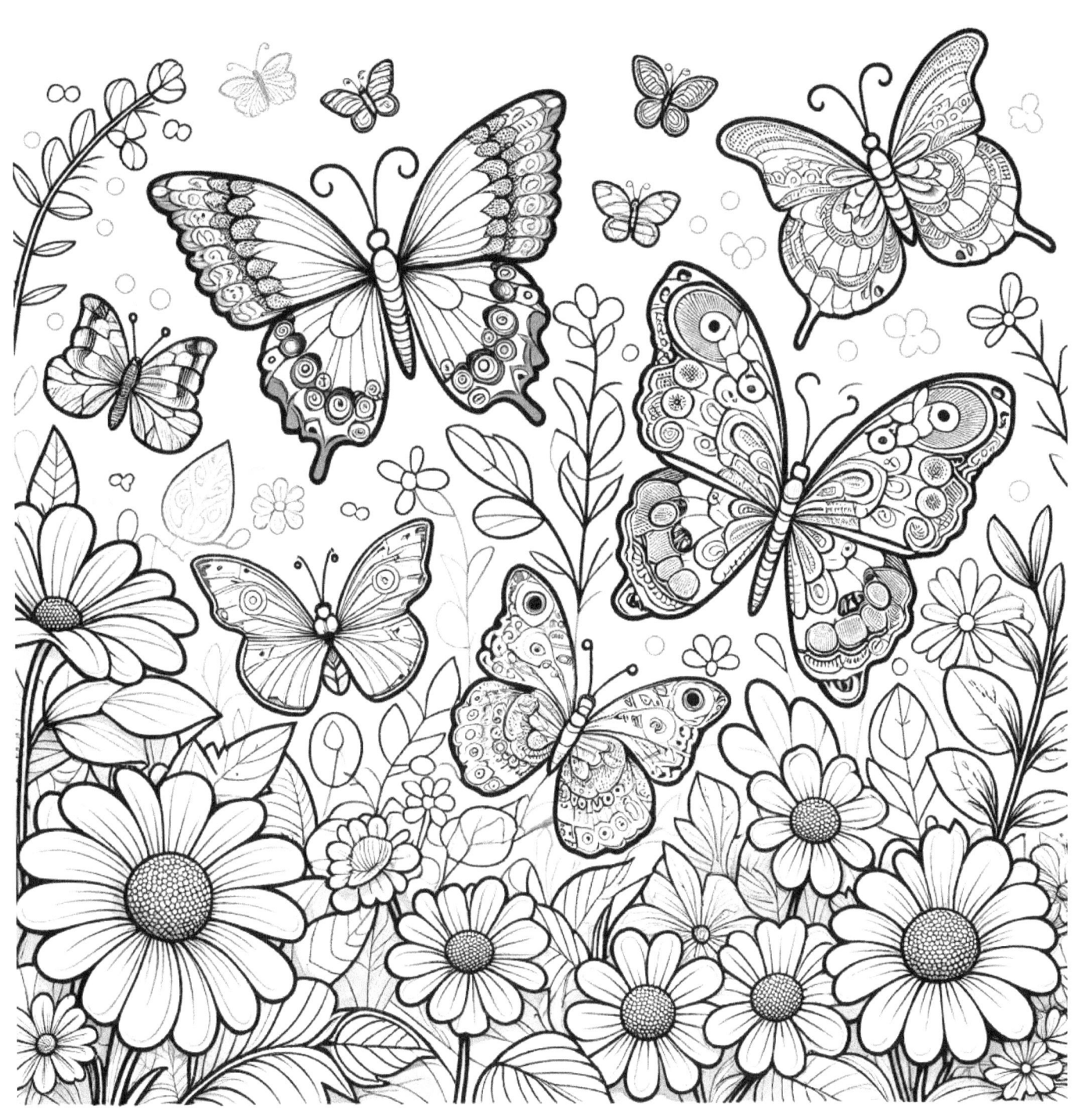

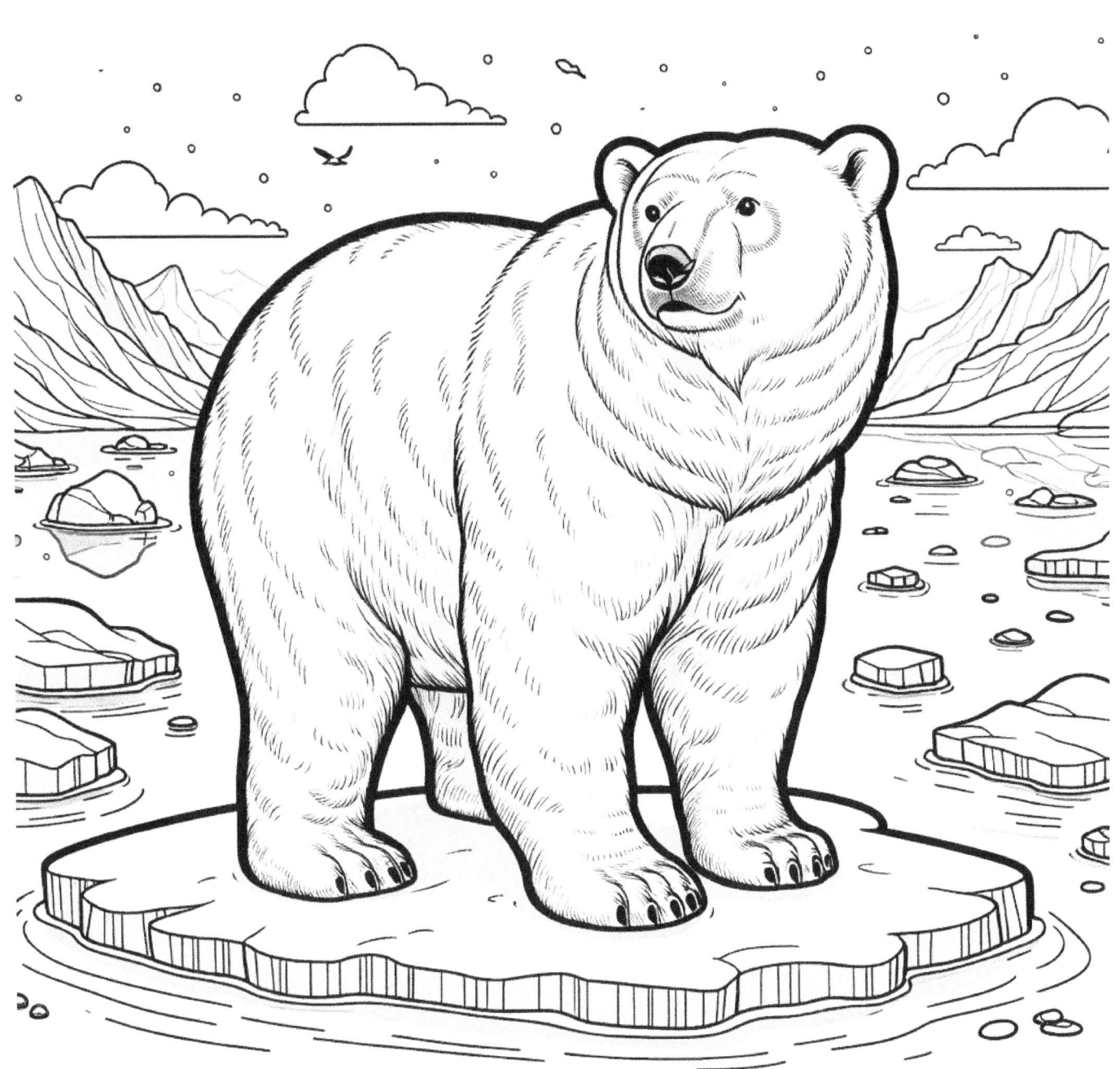

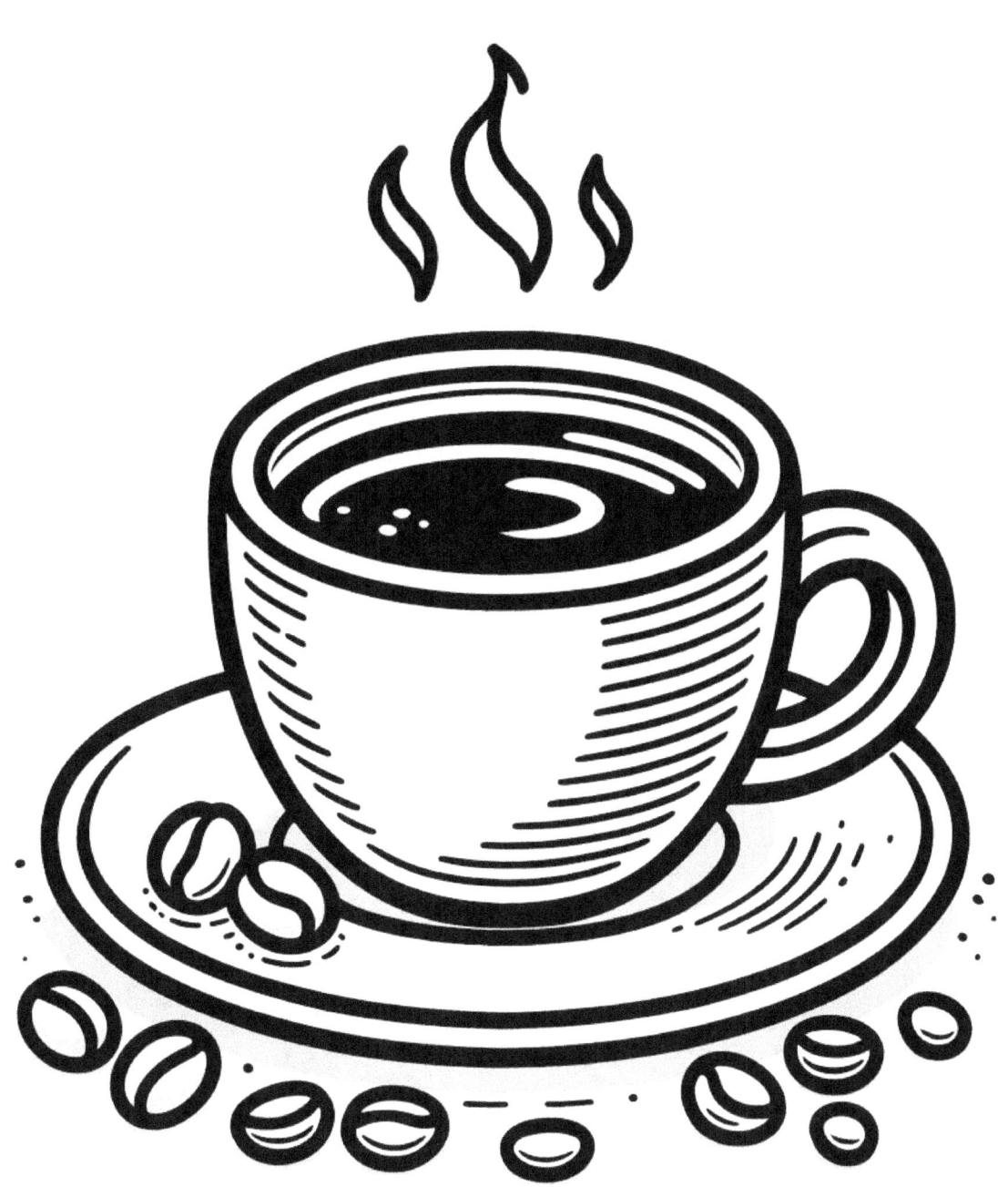

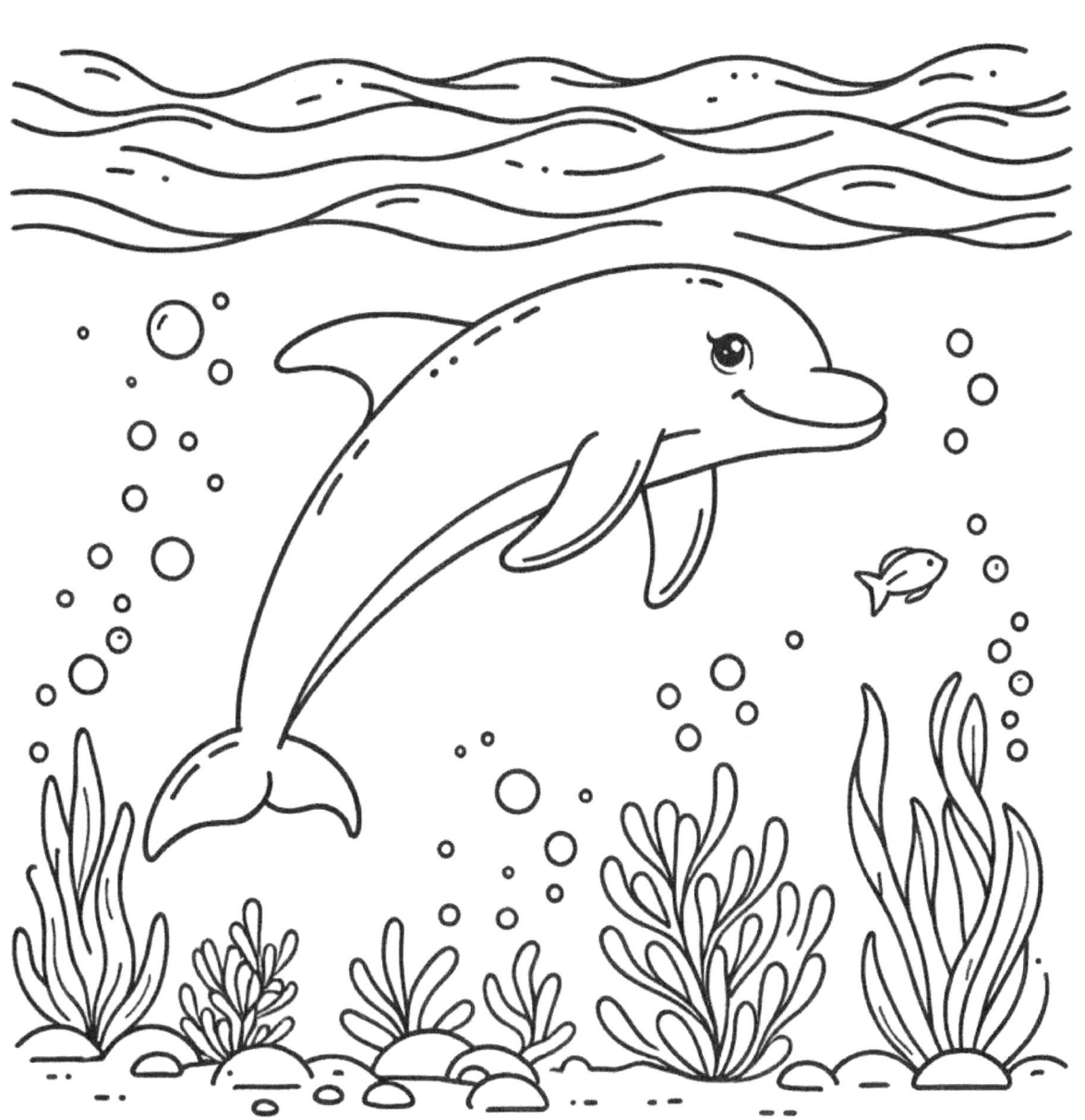

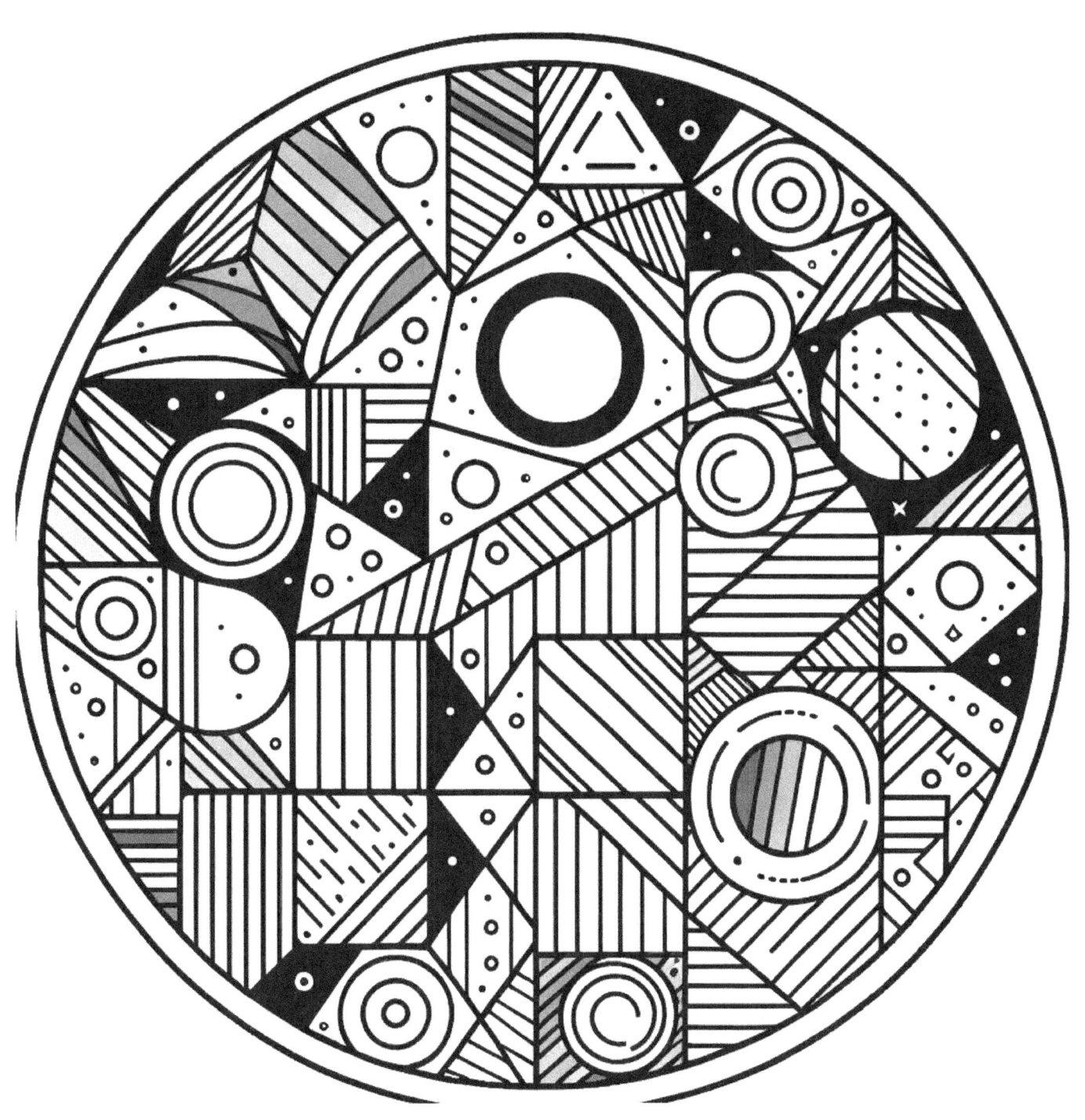

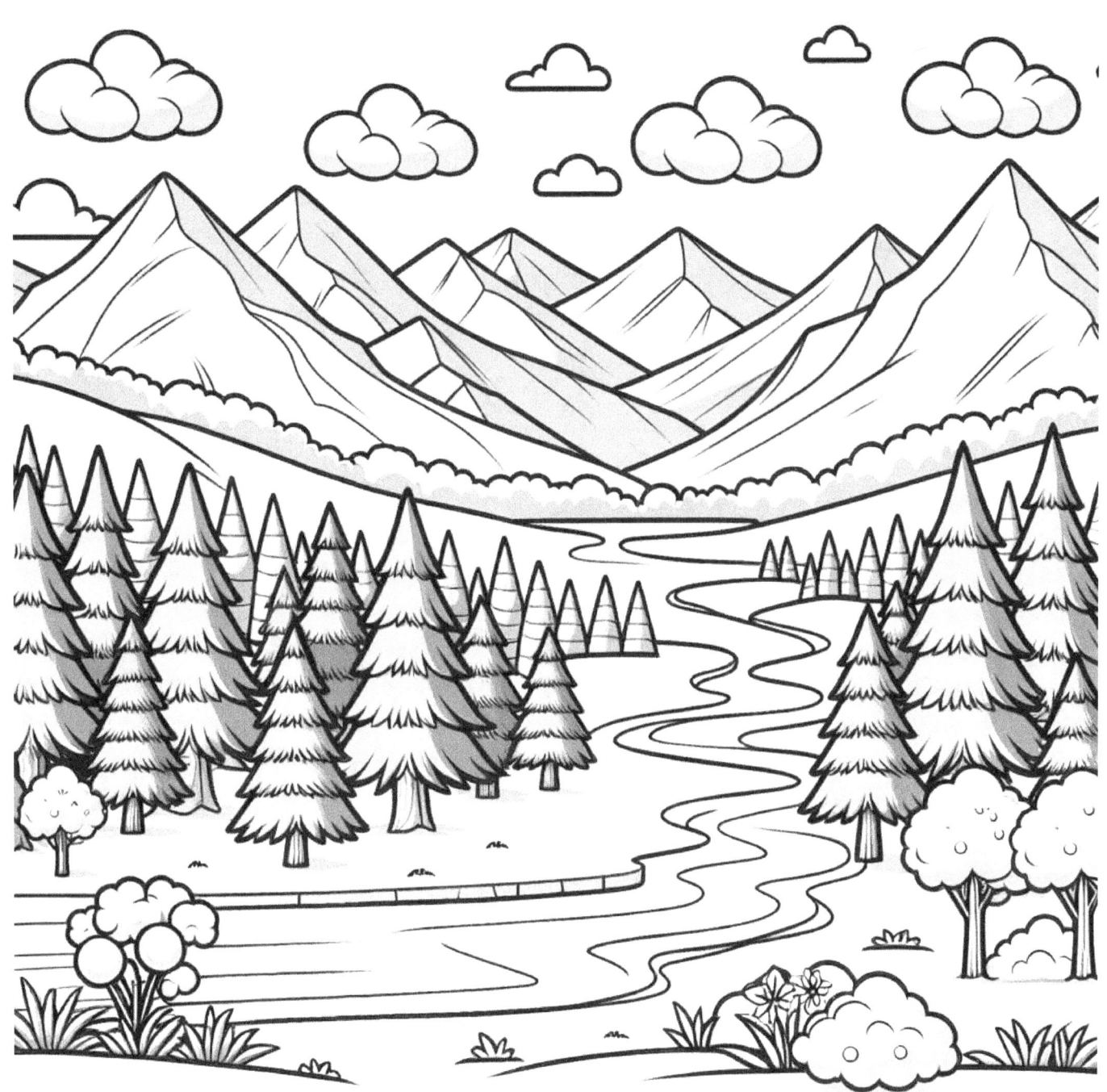

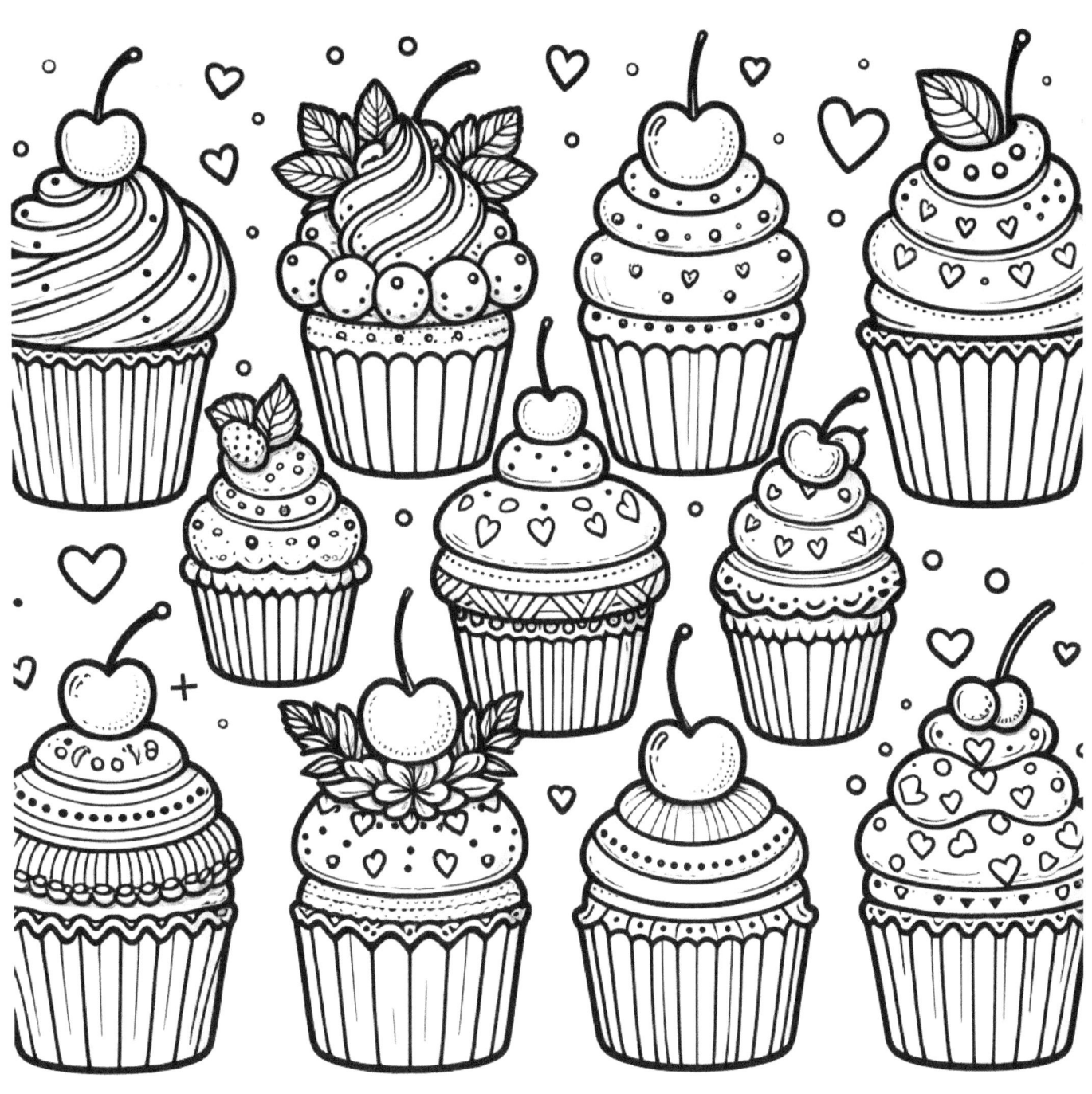

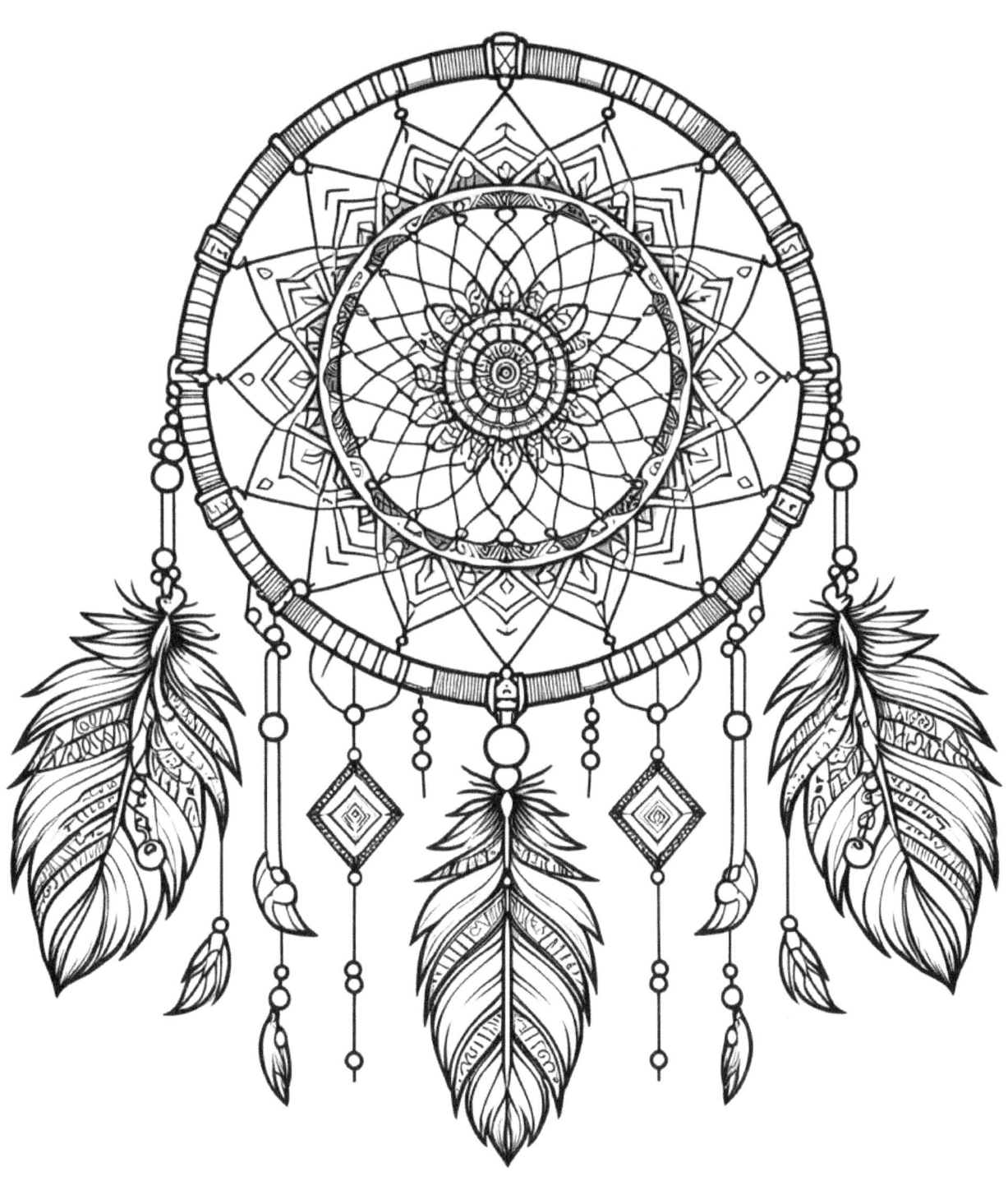

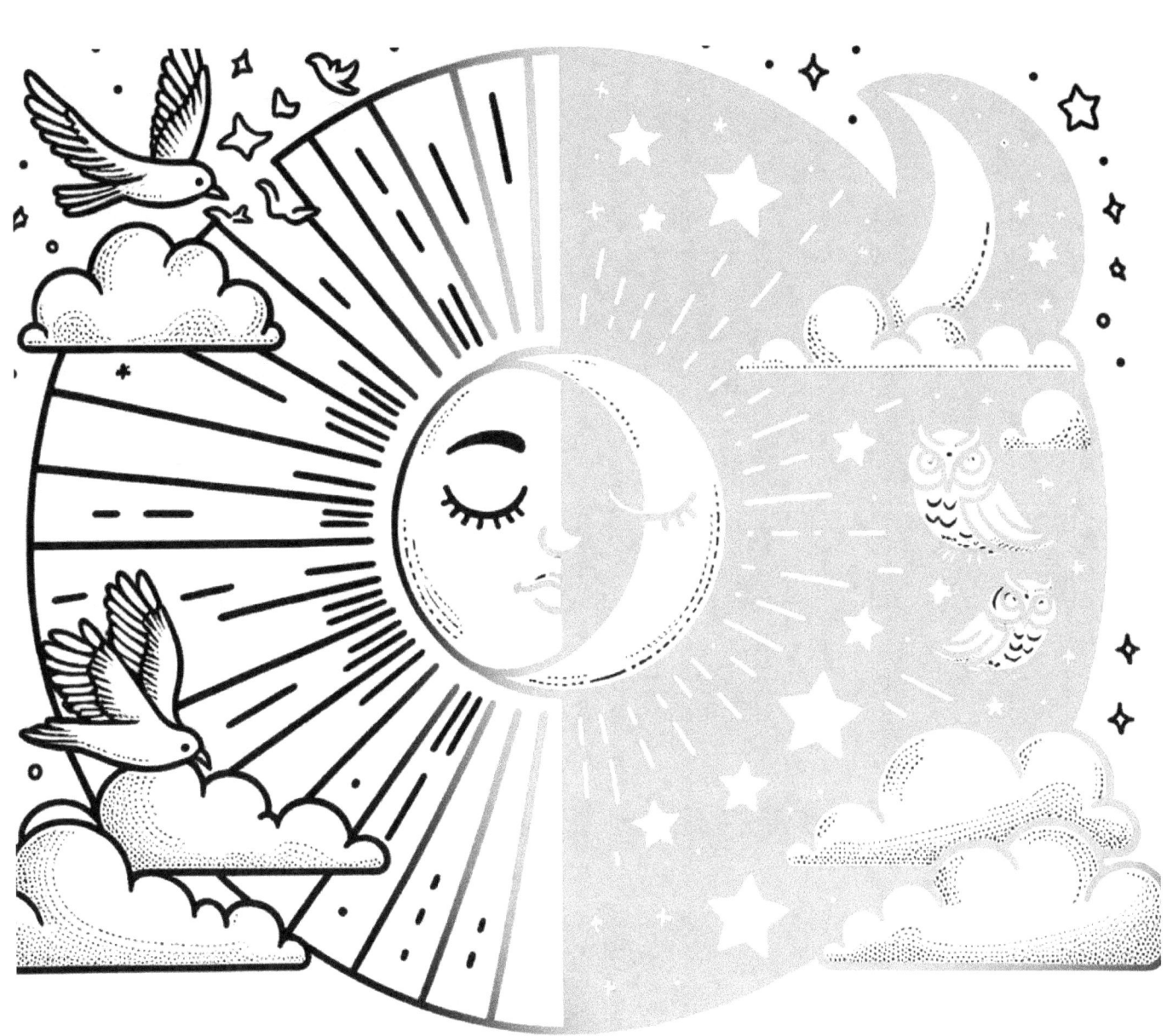

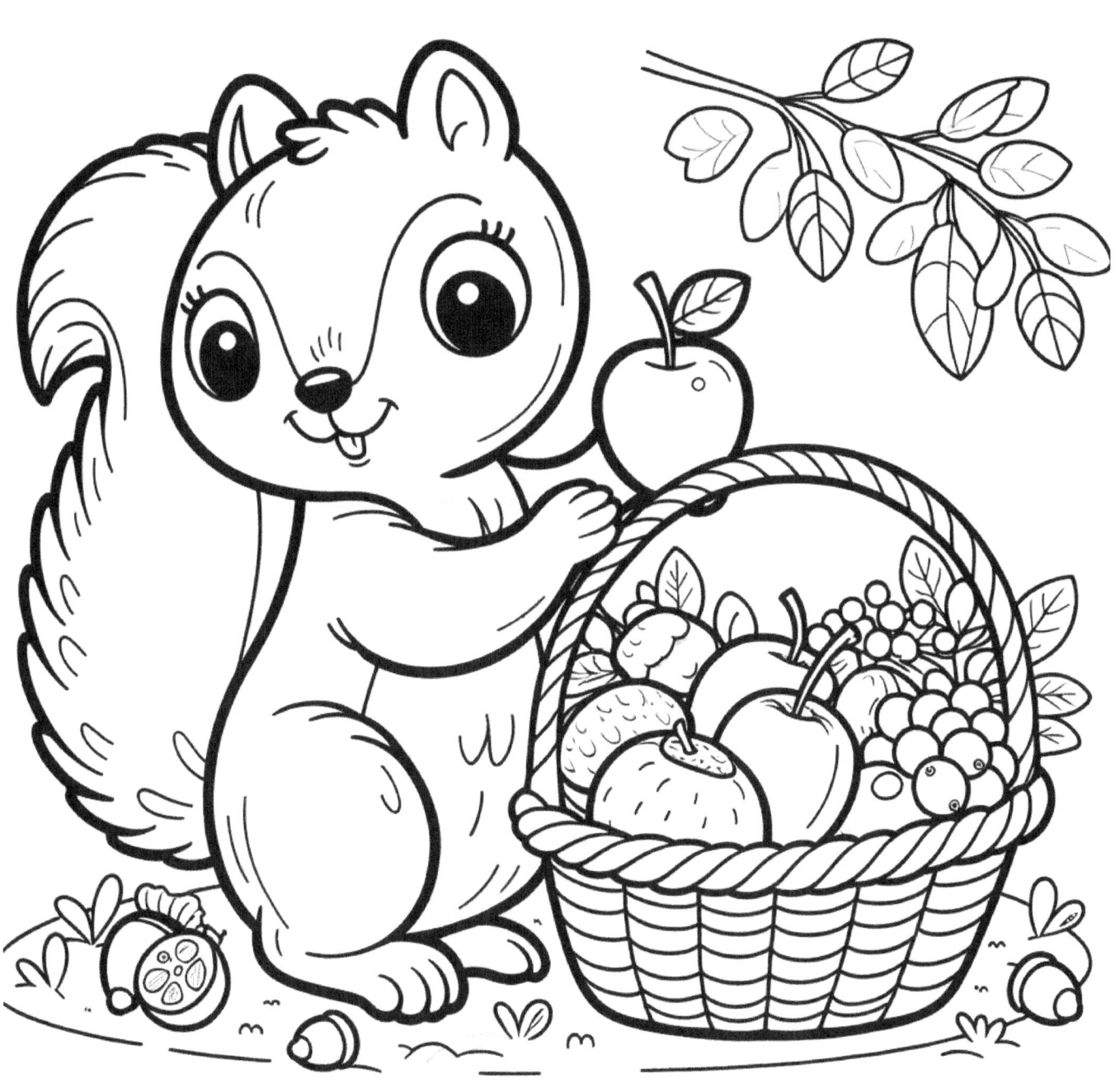

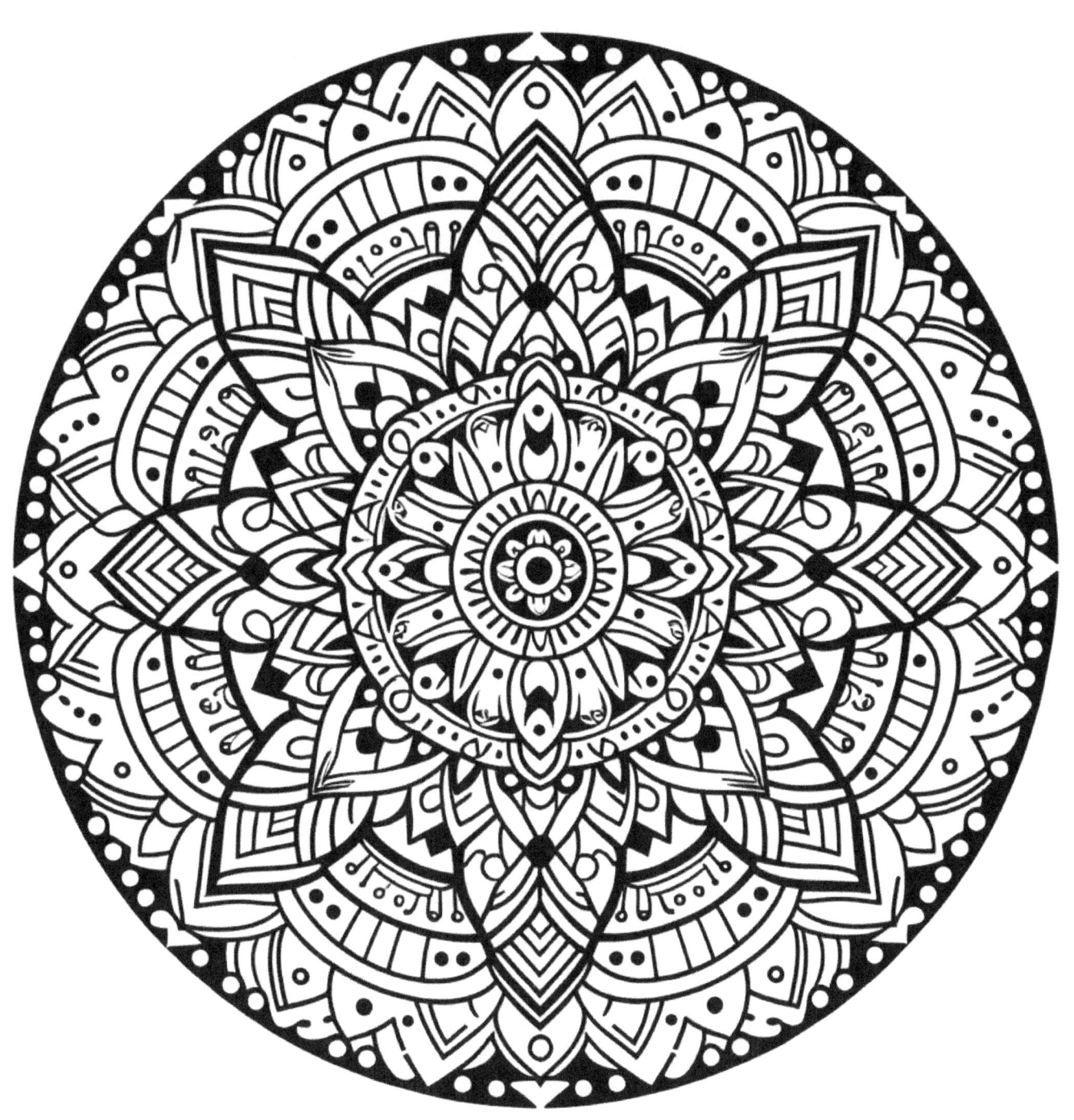

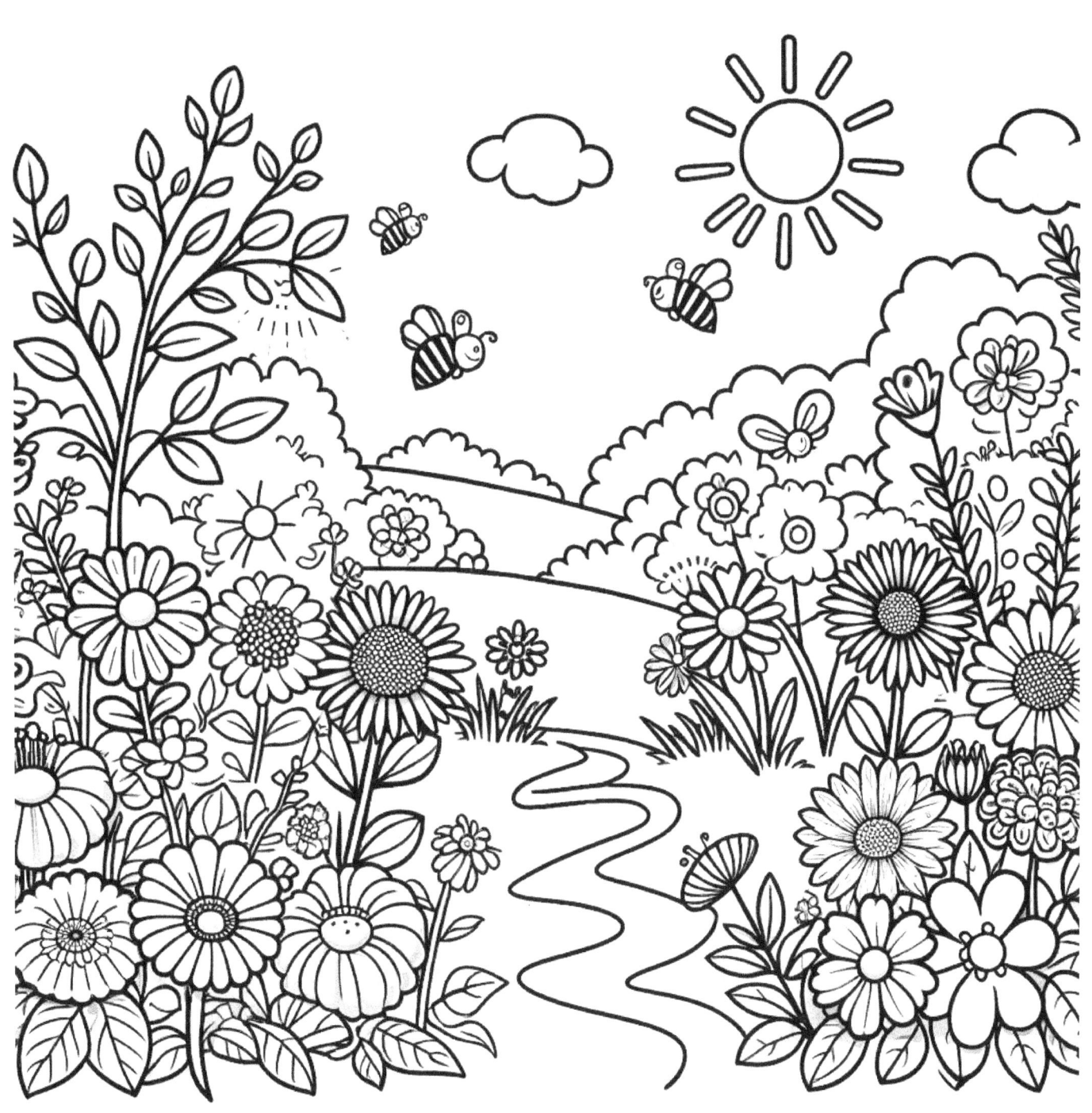

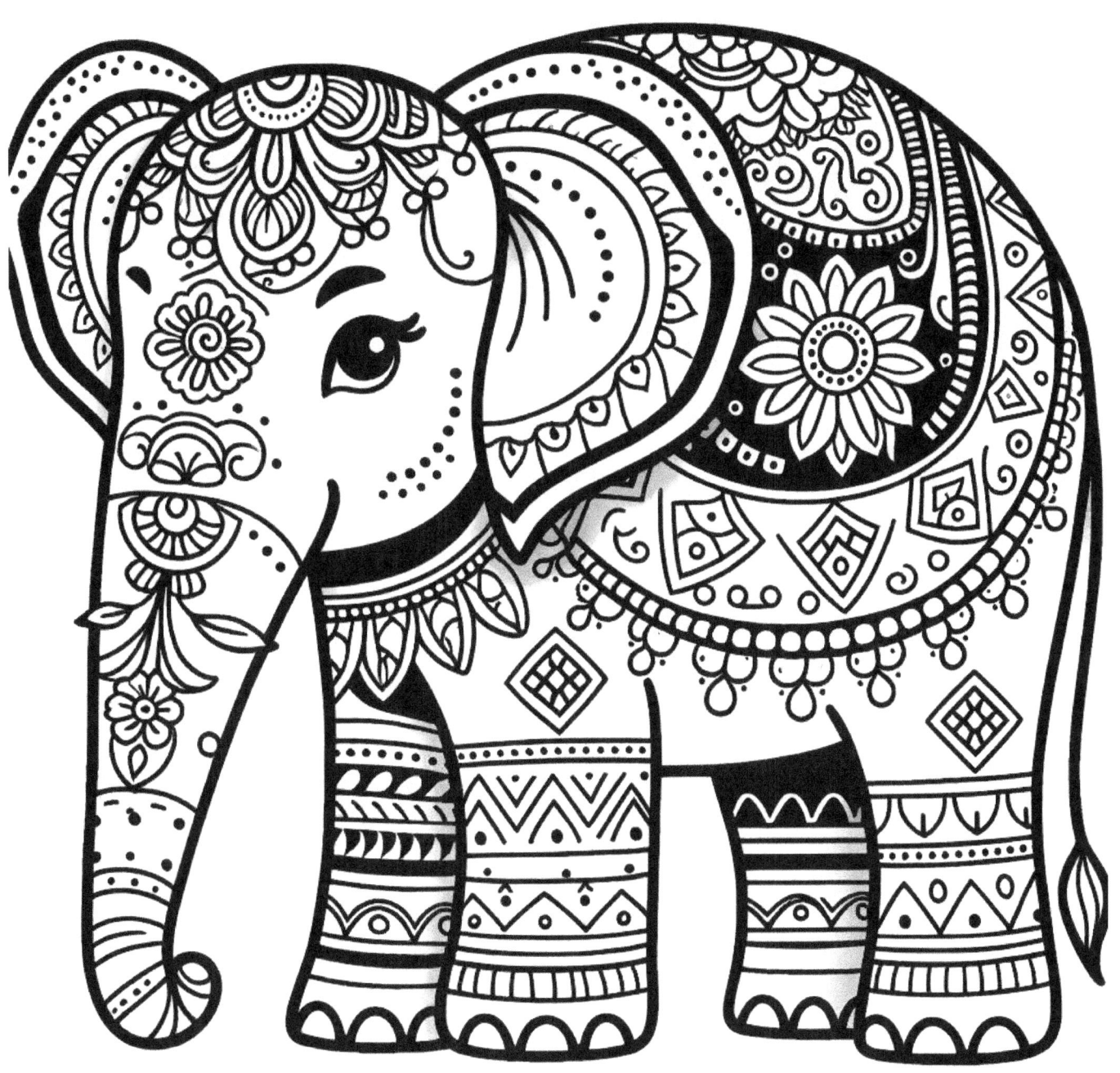

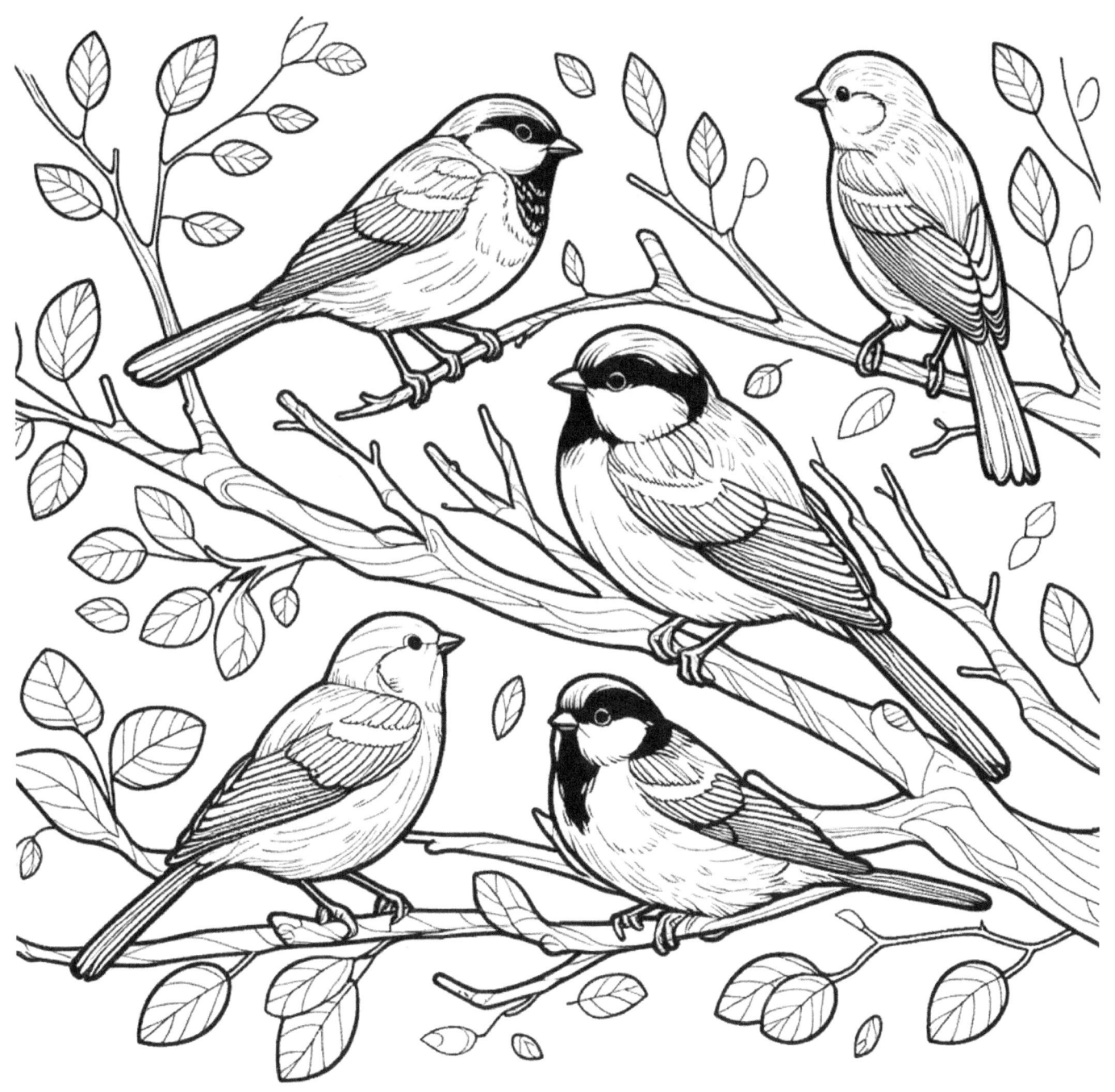

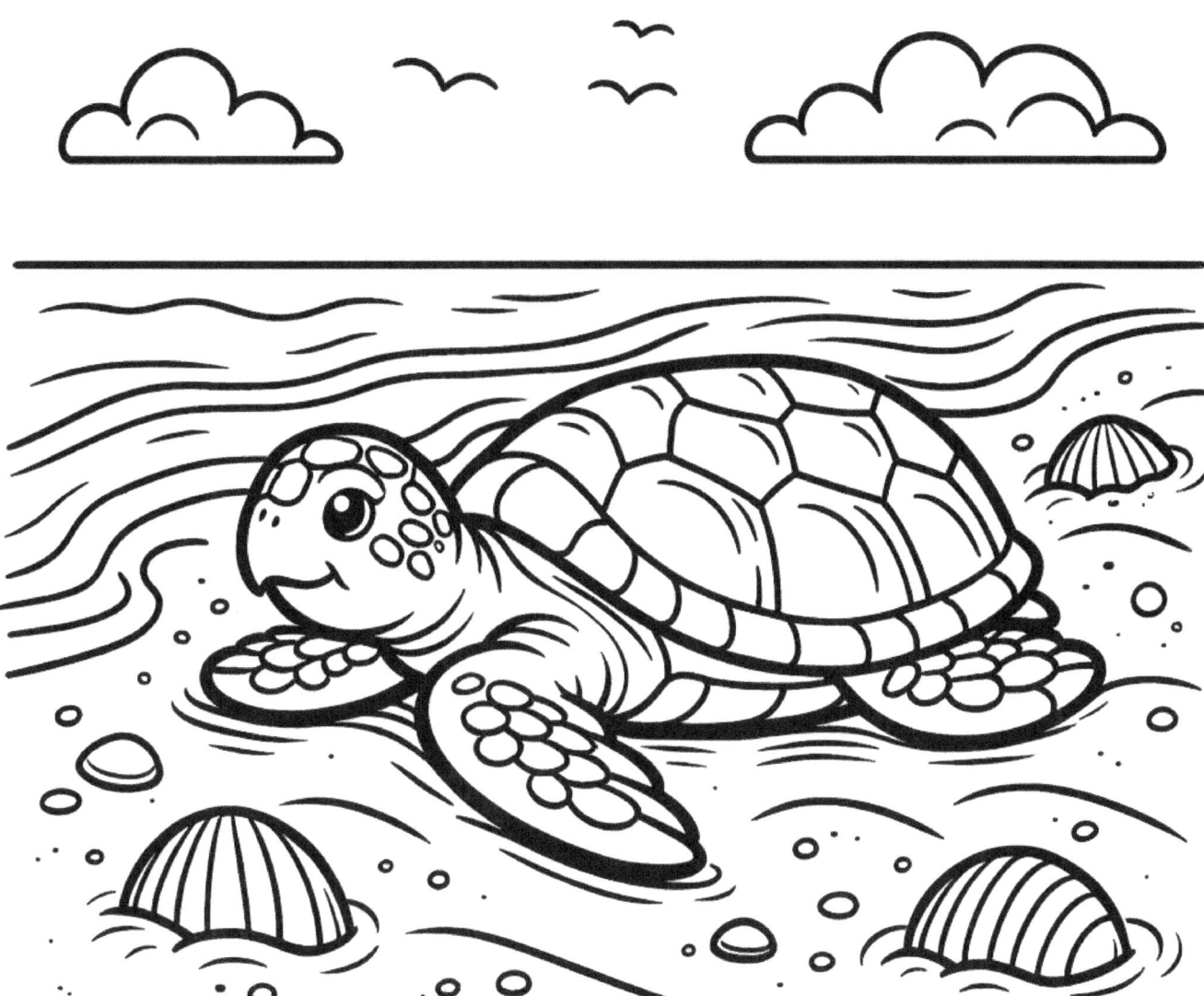

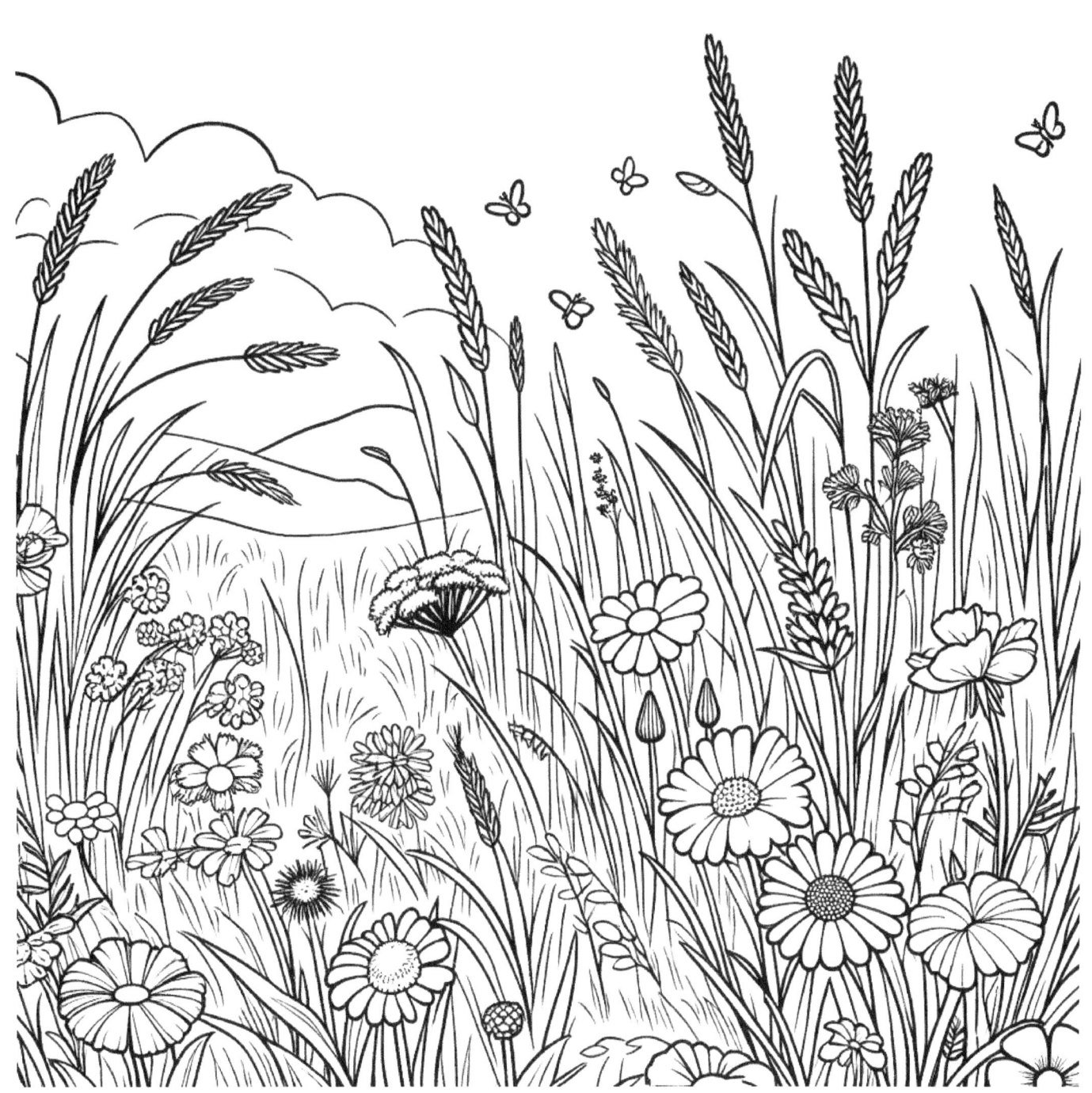

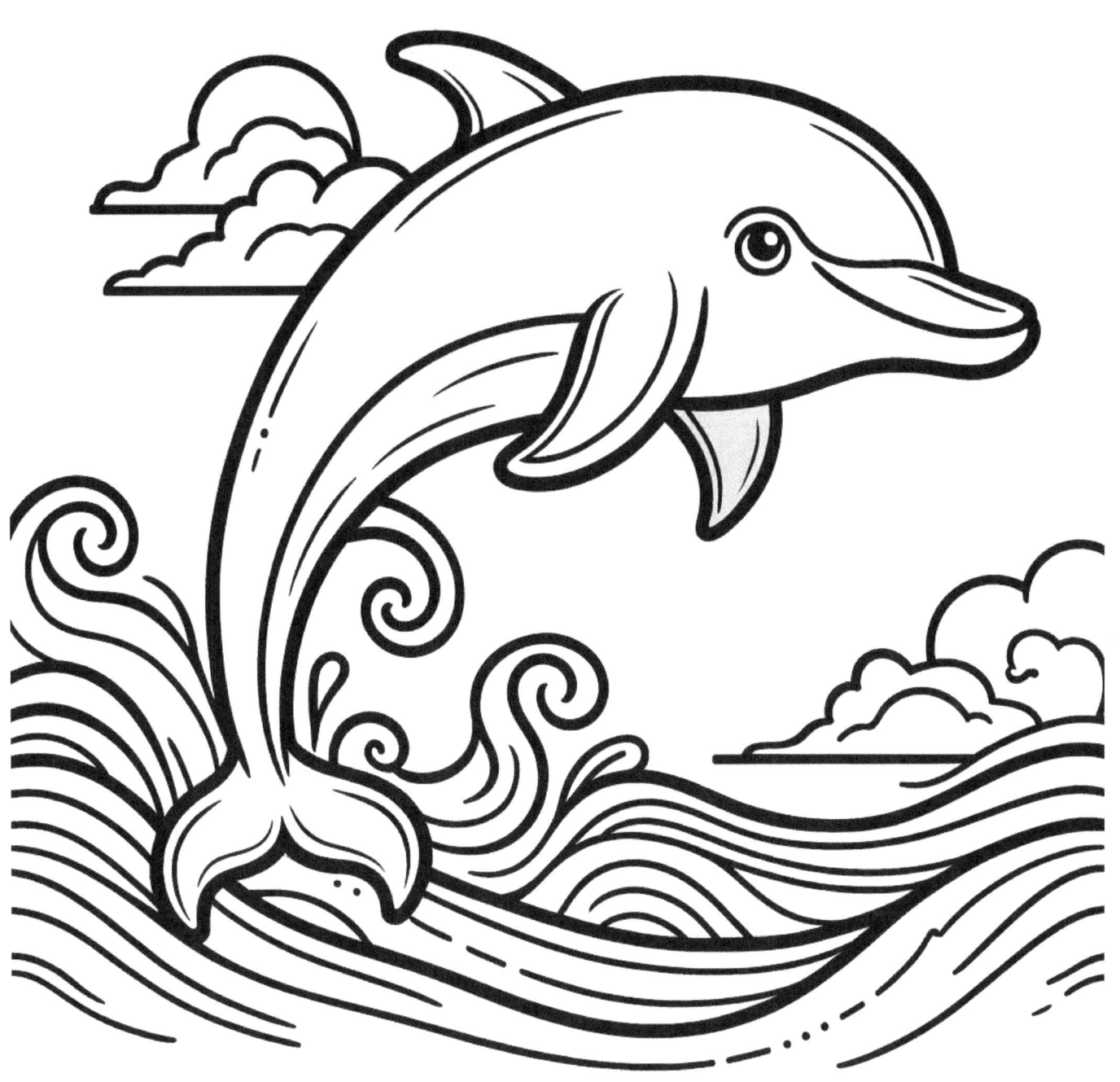

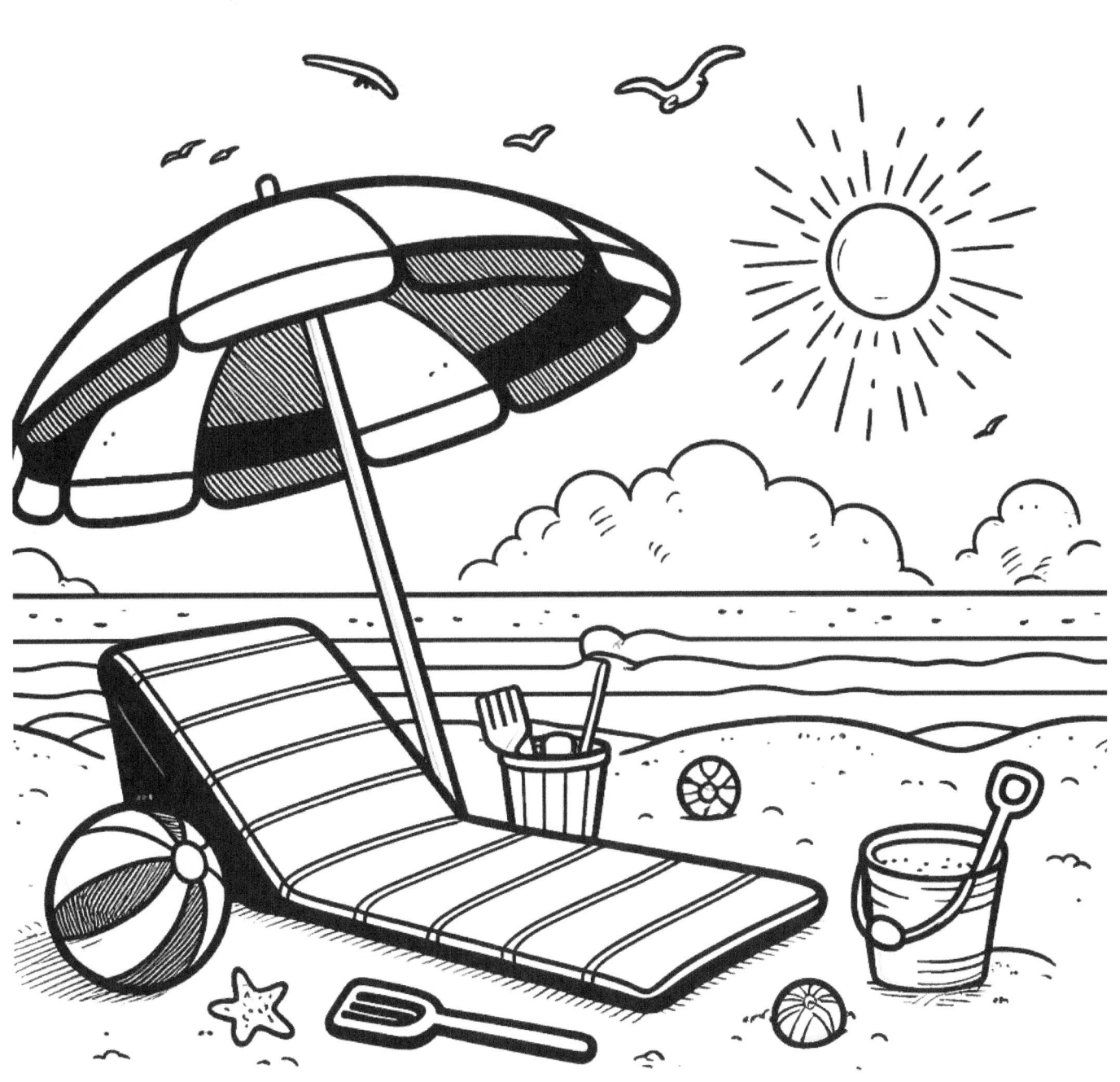

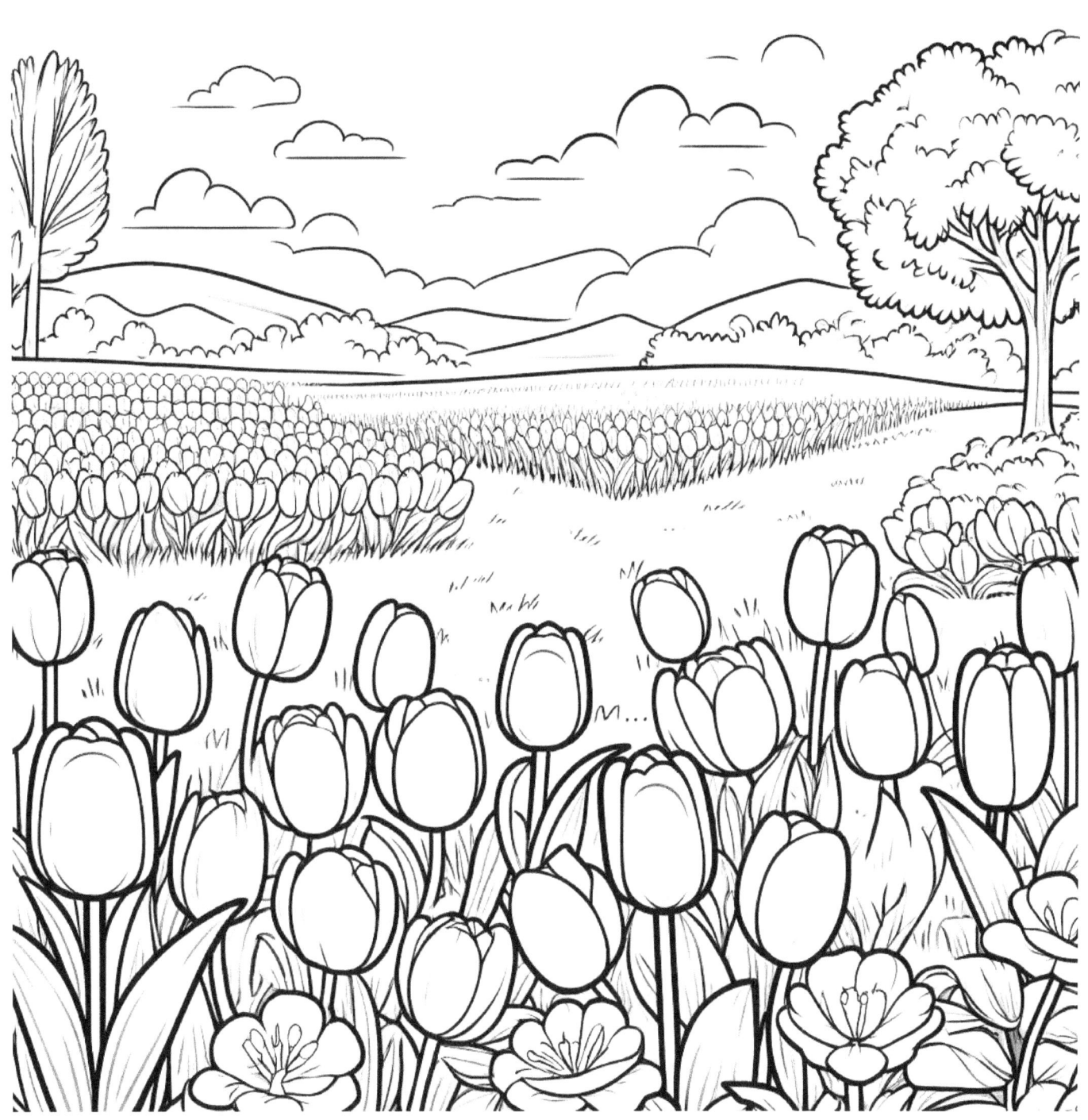

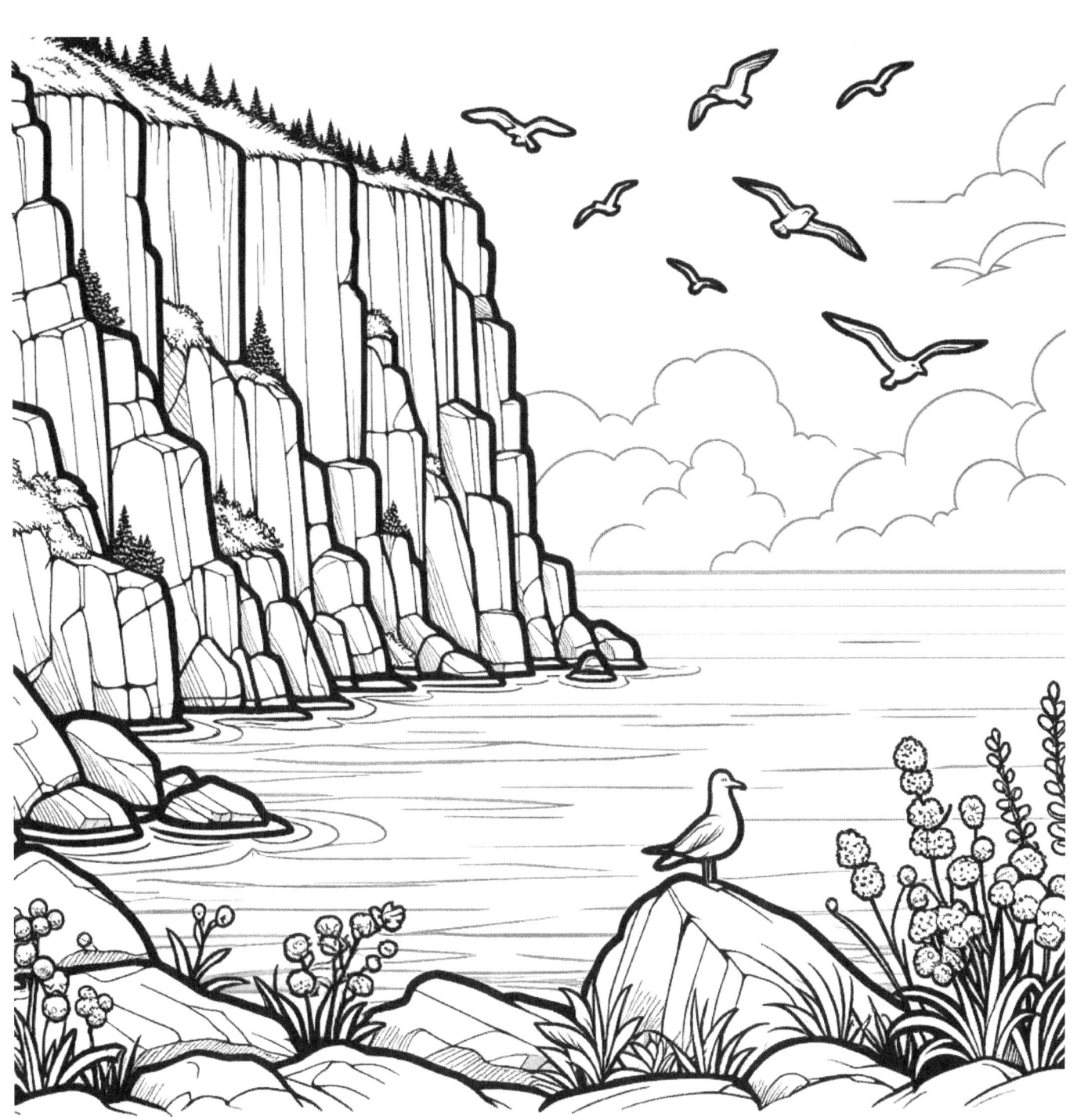

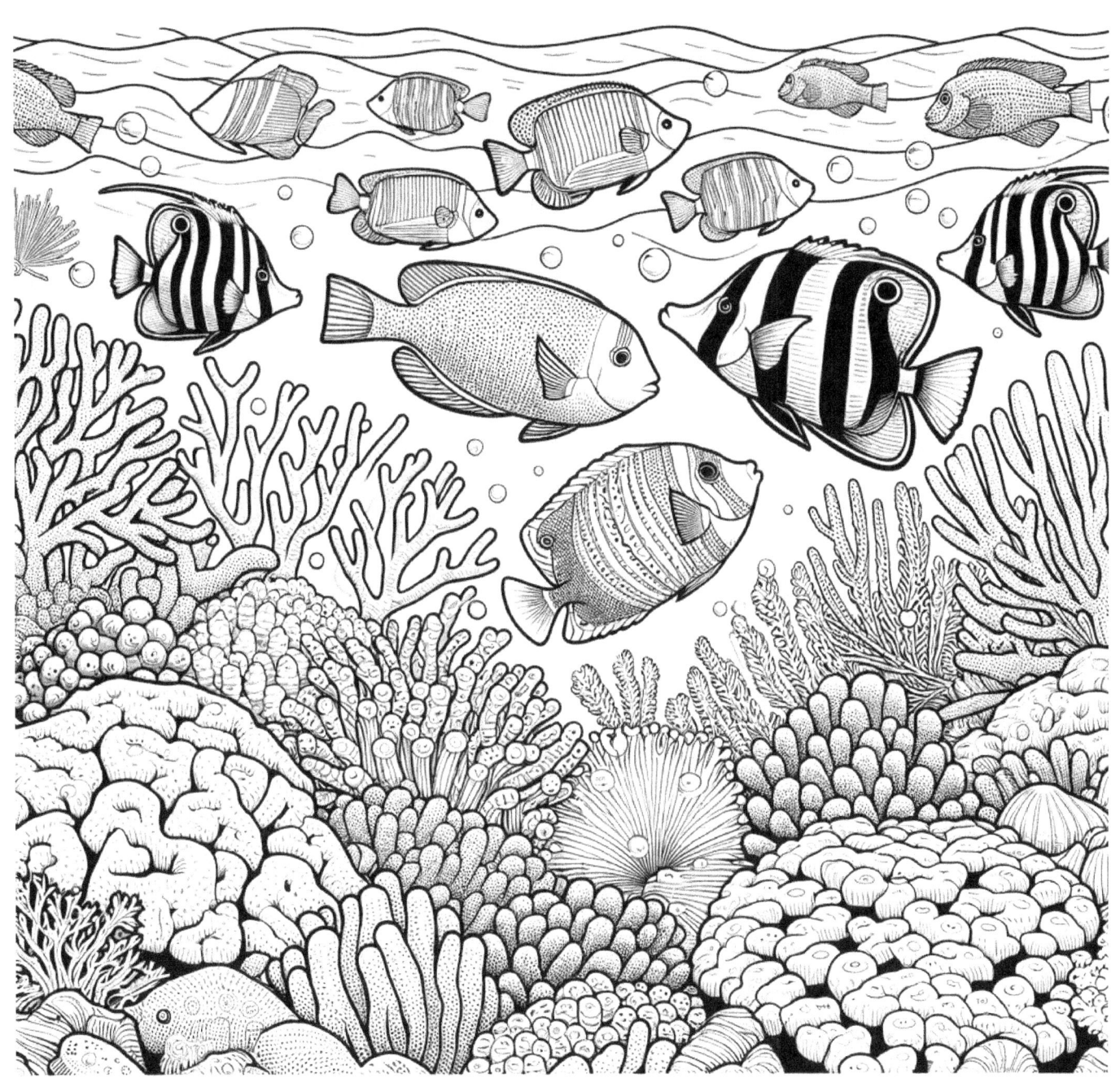

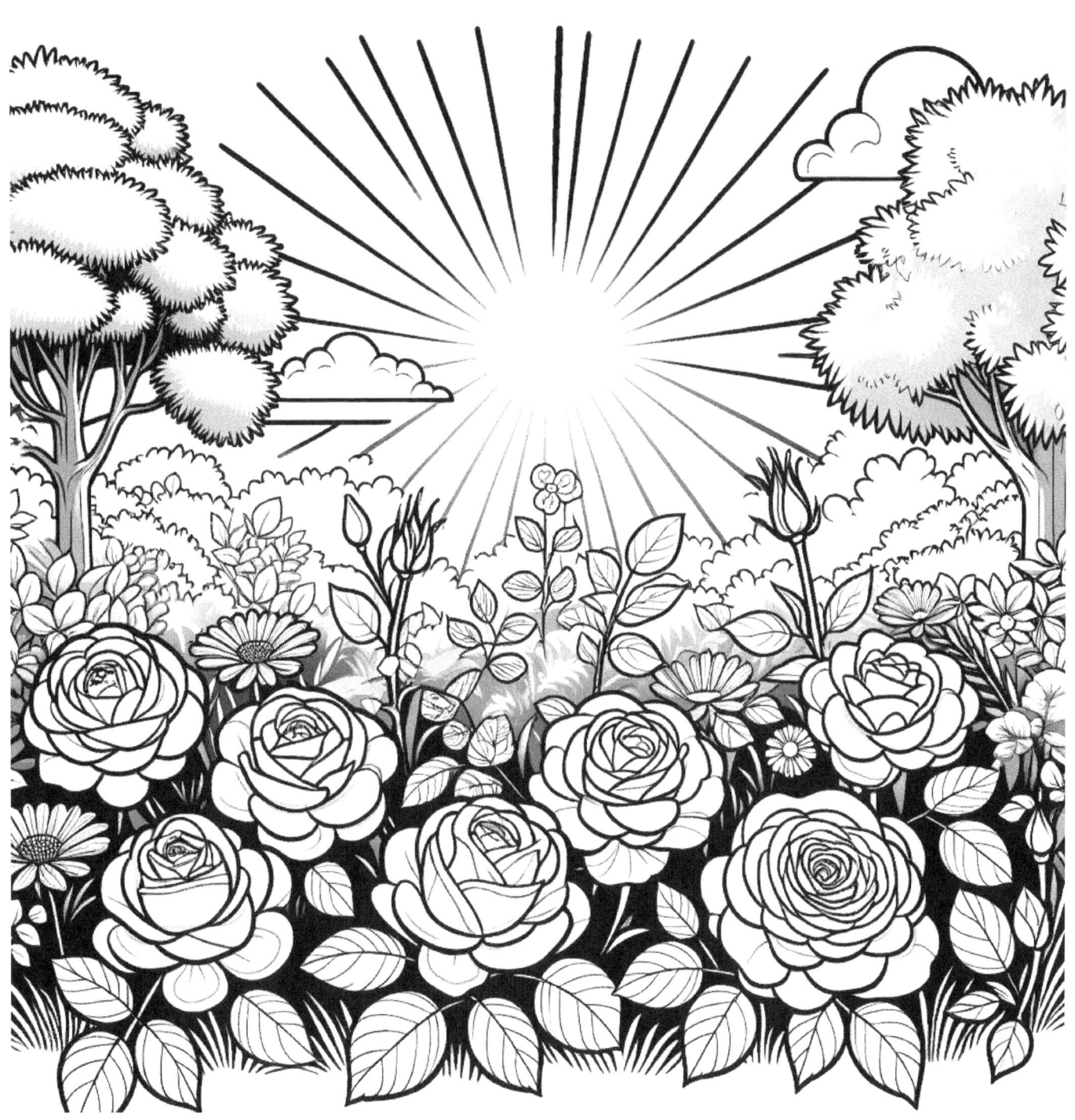

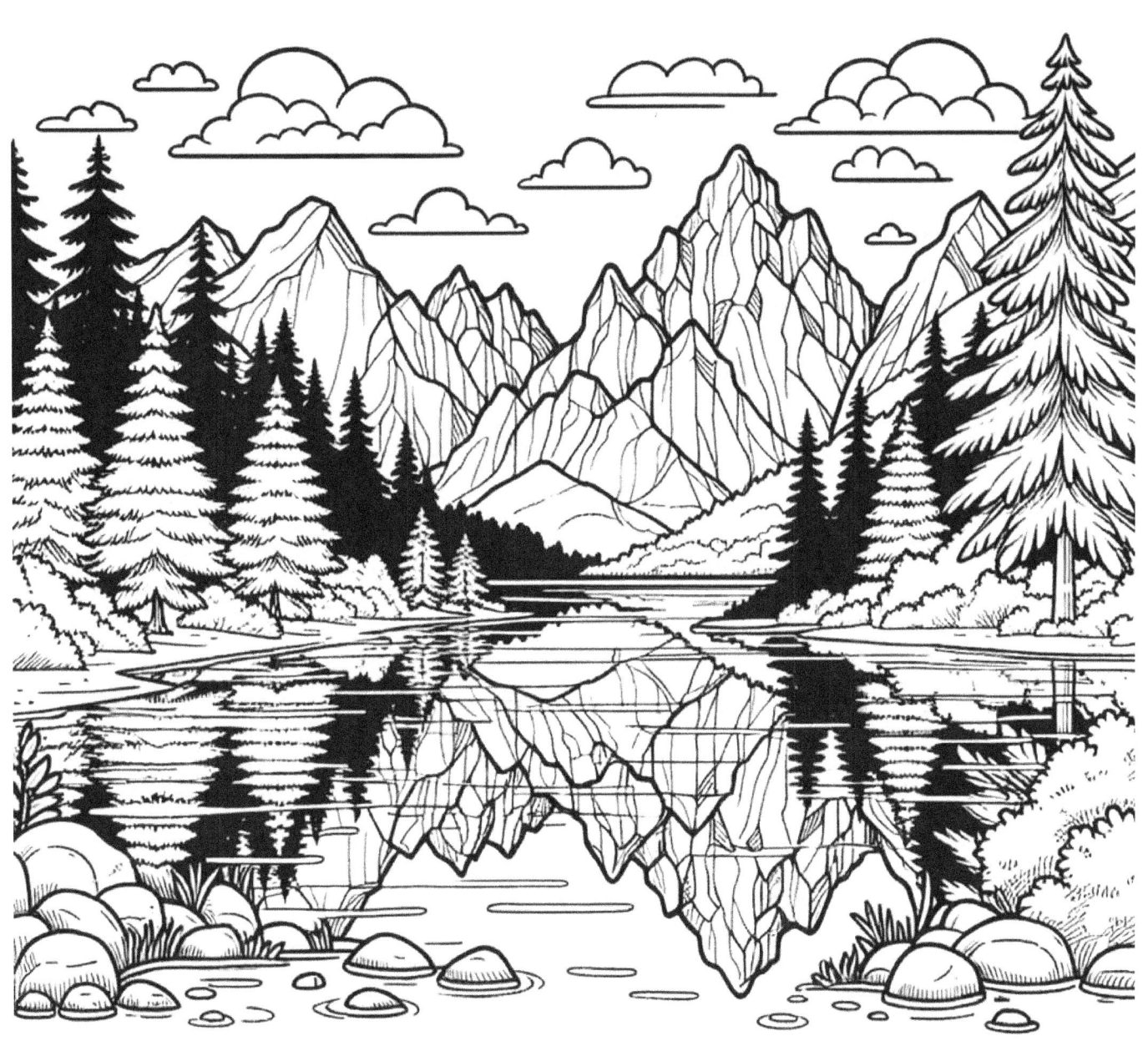

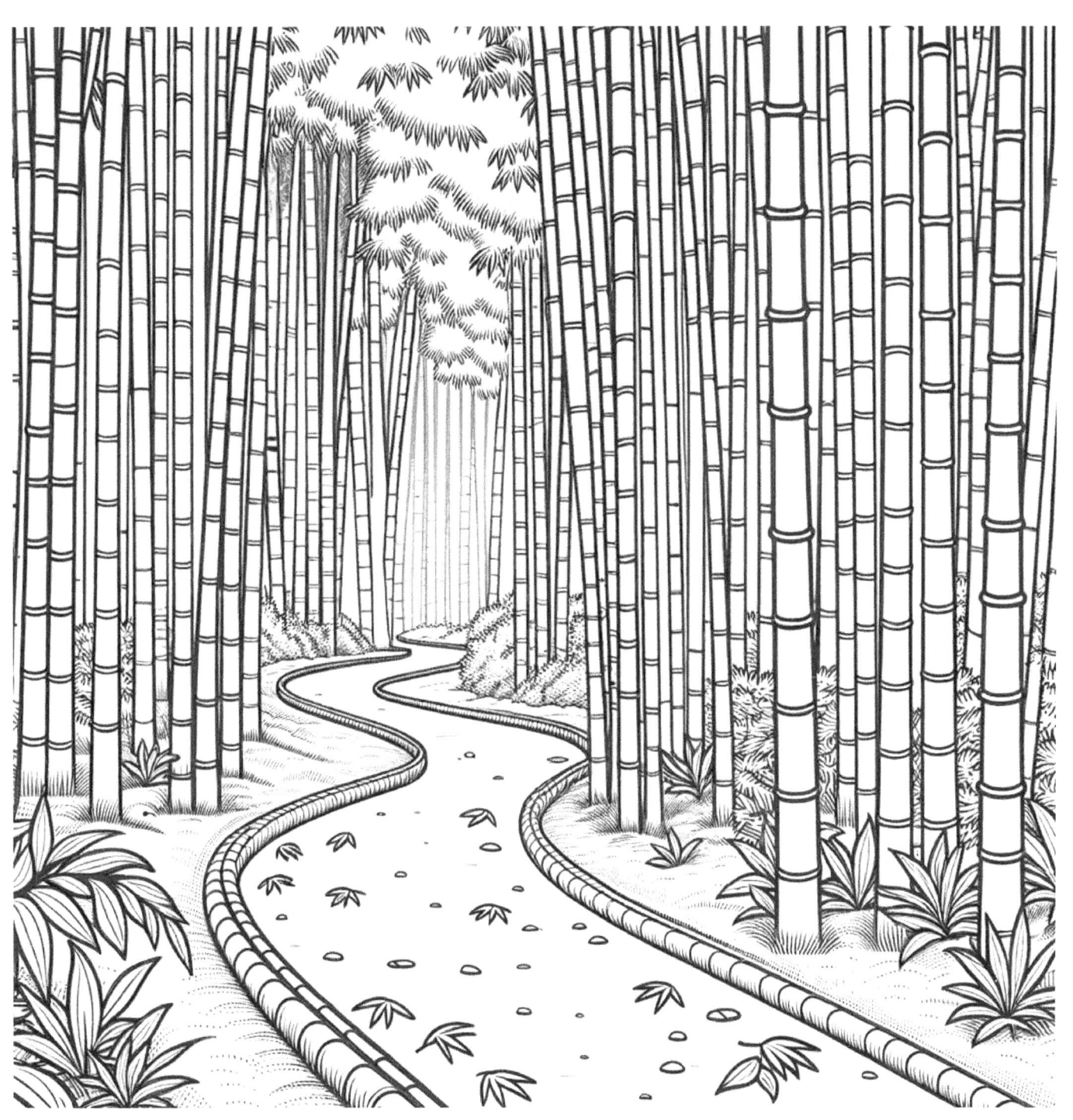

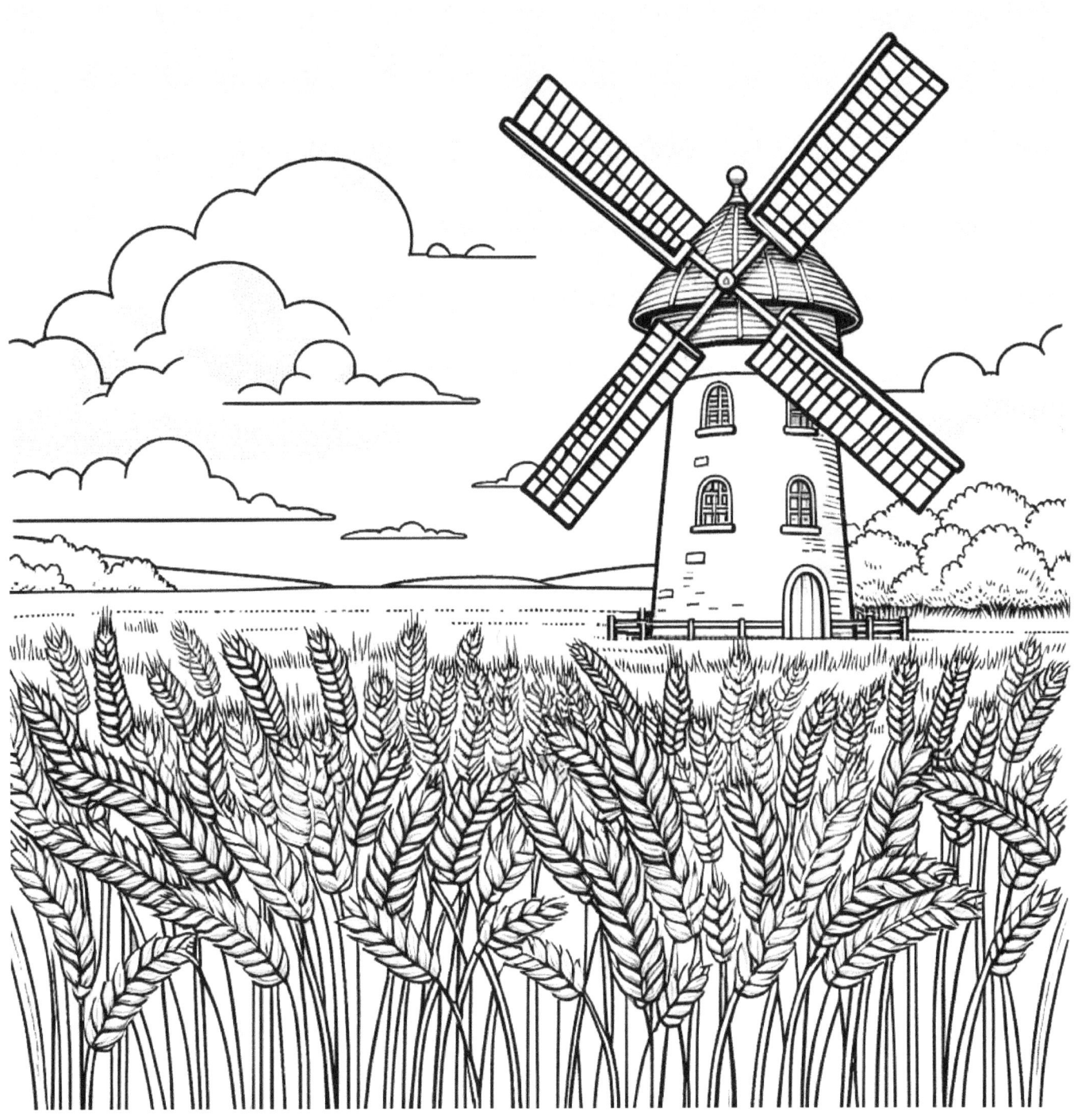

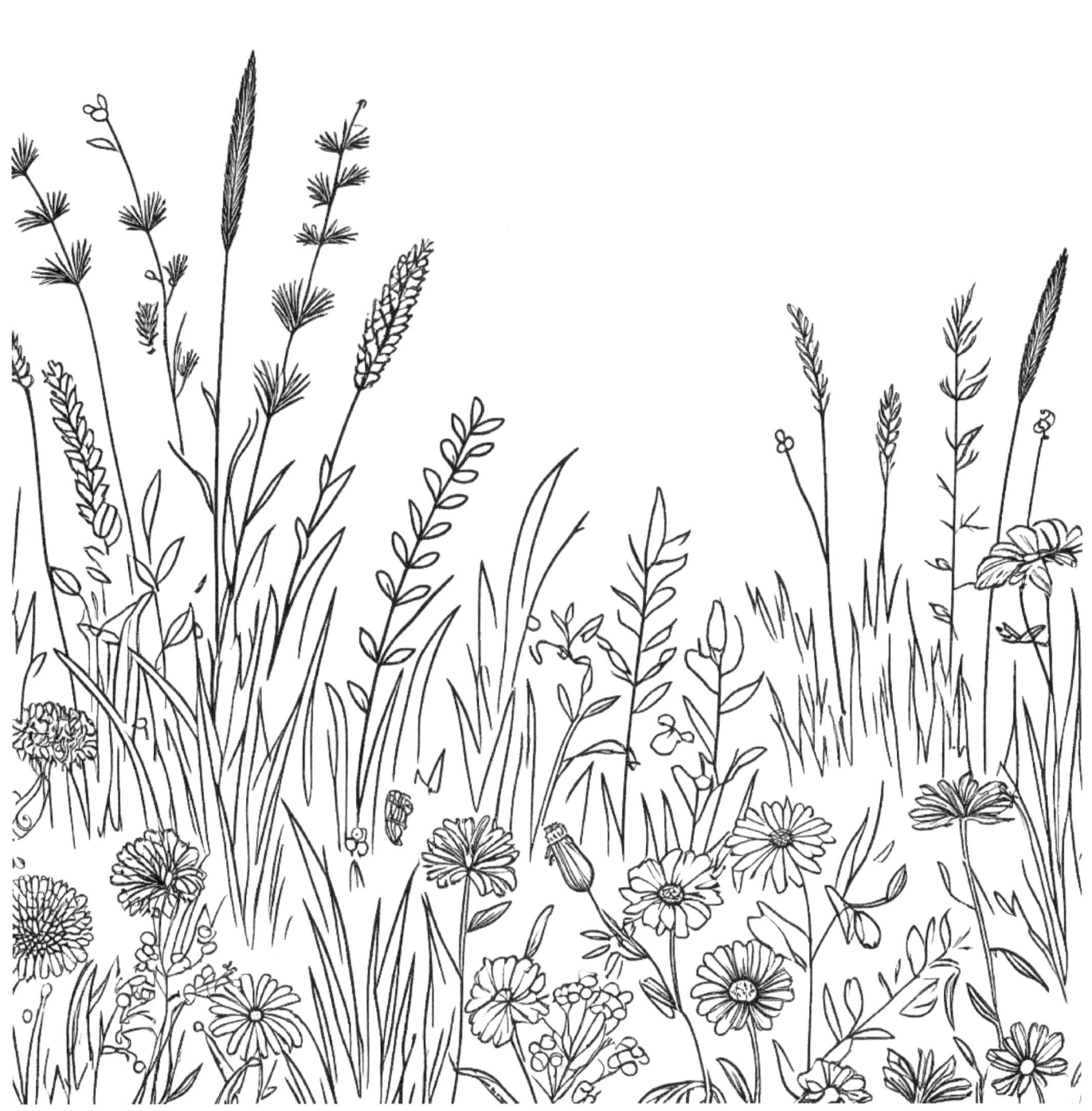

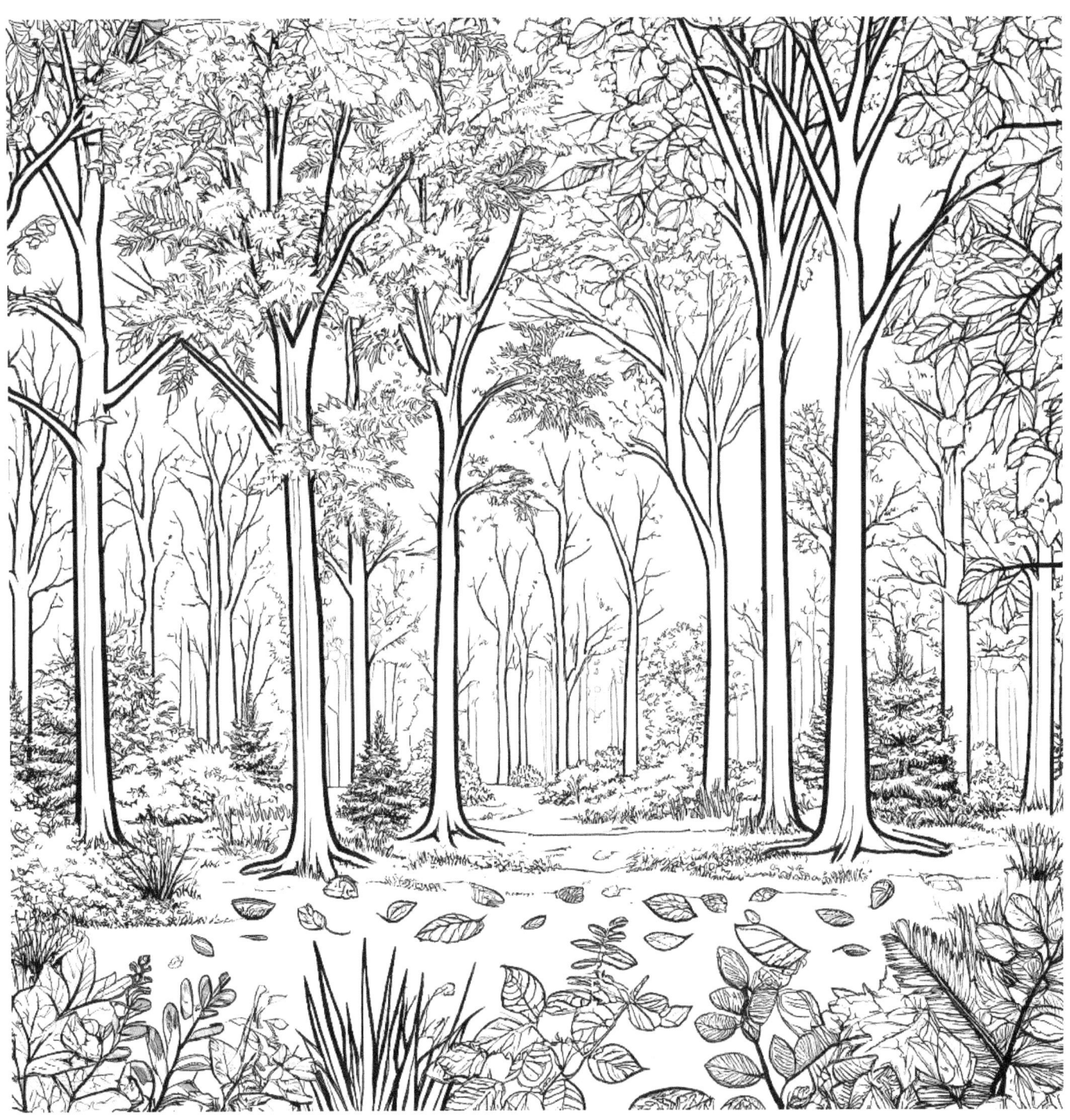

Conclusion

Thank you for buying this book, you can leave a review on Amazon saying what you liked or what you would like us to improve, until the next coloring adventure.

Pérez Arboleda

www.ingramcontent.com/pod-product-compliance
Lightning Source LLC
Chambersburg PA
CBHW062354220526
45472CB00008B/1808